# The Murder of Caroline Rose Isenberg : An Anthology of True Crime

Ruth Kanton

Published by Trellis Publishing, 2021.

THE MURDER OF CAROLINE ROSE ISENBERG : AN ANTHOLOGY OF TRUE CRIME

**First edition. July 7, 2021.**

Copyright © 2021 Ruth Kanton.

ISBN: 979-8224432189

Written by Ruth Kanton.

# THE MURDER OF CAROLINE ROSE ISENBERG

RUTH KANTON

**RUTH KANTON**

TABLE OF THE CONTENTS

Caroline Rose Isenberg was born on October 27, 1961, in Brookline, Massachusetts, to Dr. Phillip L. Isenberg and Ellin Isenberg. She was one of three kids in the family – two girls and a boy. Dr. Isenberg worked as a psychiatrist, and had his own practice in Boston. He also served as a faculty member of the Harvard Medical School. The family lived in the Brookline suburb, and Caroline graduated from Brimmer and May School in Chestnut Hill, Massachusetts, in 1980. She enrolled in Harvard after graduation, where she majored in Fine Arts, and according to her mother, she was an excellent student. Caroline lived in Currier House while at Harvard, and was active in various clubs, all in line with her theatrical pursuits. She joined the Harvard Independent Theater, the Harvard-Radcliffe Dramatic House, and the Lowell House Dramatic Society. She starred in various student productions, including "Who's Afraid of Virginia Woolf," "Twelfth Night," and "The Glass Menagerie." She was also in "Measure for Measure," an American Repertory Theater's production.

The literary director of the American Repertory Theater, Jonathan Marks, spoke about Caroline, stating, "She was very promising." He recalled watching "The Glass Menagerie" in 1983, in which Caroline had played the character Laura. He stated that there was a "sweet shyness" in Caroline's portrayal of the character, and that "She was determined to be an actress." In the summer of 1984, Caroline spent her time in Williamston, Massachusetts, for the summer stock theater. In the fall, she moved to New York to further pursue her acting career.

**The Apartment Building**

929 West End Avenue featured 30 apartments spanning its seven floors when Caroline and her roommate, Susan Glassman, moved into apartment 7-C on October 10, 1984. The building itself was an old gray brick structure with a limestone base. Like the other small apartment buildings in the area, it featured minimal security system – just a front door lock and buzzer system. However, the lock was problematic, and was not necessarily reliable. One tenant, singer Dian

Blomquist, said: "Sometimes the front-door lock works and sometimes it doesn't. The tenants have written to the management about the lock, but it never does any good. With a hard enough push, anybody can get in. I'm sure that's the way the killer got in." Past the front door was a dimly lit 15-foot lobby. This featured faded yellow walls and dirty tiled floors. There were four corridors leading into the lobby, relatively hidden from the front door. About eight feet from the front door is a self-service elevator, which had a black door. The interior of the elevator featured imitation wood Formica, and was only lit with a single dim light bulb.

Noreen Williams, a resident of the building who lived on the sixth floor, described the elevator, "There was one little light bulb in the elevator; the other three were burned out. It's a very slow elevator, and if you press a floor, you can't get another floor until you stop at the first one. If you hit the roof floor, then no other floor will work." The final stop for the elevator was a small roof structure where the elevator shaft was located. Just outside the elevator door was a six foot long hallway leading up to rust colored metal door, which was only secured by a slip-bolt on the inside. The hallway was lit by a single dim bulb. On the other side of the door was the 25 foot by 50 foot roof, whose illumination came from the faint lights from the windows of the neighboring taller buildings.

**Attack and Death**

Once in New York, Caroline enrolled at the Neighborhood Playhouse School of the Theater, located at 340 East 54th Street. Her mother said in an interview, "She wanted to be in the theater in many ways - acting, directing, any way she could. She was a gregarious, outgoing, warmhearted person. She felt so good about going to that school." On December 1, 1984, Caroline spent her evening watching a Broadway show, and later had dinner at a restaurant before heading home. She made her way through the building's front door, but never made it into her apartment. In the dimly lit elevator, Caroline was accosted by a man, who brandished a knife and told her to shut up, and threatened to kill her if she made any sound. He then pressed the top floor button of the elevator. As they made their way to the top, the man robbed her, taking the money that was in her purse. He walked her onto the roof of the building, planning to rape her. However, Caroline resisted the man's advances, repeatedly refusing his requests to have sex with her. This sparked a frenzied attack.

At 1:30 a.m., Noreen Williams, the sixth floor resident, heard piercing screams: "There was a hell of a struggle up there. I heard the whole thing, but there was nothing I could do about it. There was nothing anybody could do about it. She was leaning over the roof edge, screaming for help, screaming: 'He's stabbing me! He's going to kill me! I'm bleeding to death! Help me!' I couldn't see her. It was too dark. I called the police as soon as I heard the screaming. The police operator could hear the screams. The police were here almost immediately, but he must have just got away over the other roof." Uniformed officers from the 24th precinct quickly responded to Williams' call, and were on the scene within minutes. In her account of the night's events, resident Dian Blomquist stated: "She said his words were, 'Will you have sex with me?' and she said, 'No, I will not,' and that's when he started stabbing her. She must have started screaming then. He started stabbing her, many times, in the chest. When we heard the screams, every light in this building and the next went on. All up and down the lights were flipping on, and people were looking out their windows trying to figure out where they were coming from."

While officers were on the way to the scene, the assailant abruptly stopped his attack, jumped over two foot barrier onto the roof of the adjacent seven story building. From the building at 300 West 106th Street, on the corner of West End Avenue, he had four possible routes of escape – a door which led to the interior stairwell, and three fire escapes around the building's exterior. The responding officers rushed into 925 West End Avenue at the corner of 105th Street and made their way up to the roof. They searched the roof, and quickly realized that they had responded to the wrong building. They were just south of the correct building, as their flashlights were trained on Caroline. There was a five foot air shaft gap between the two buildings, and Noreen Williams recalled: "They shined flashlights over onto this roof and saw her. She was yelling out, '929! 929!' and they yelled, 'Wait a minute! Wait a minute!'" They rushed to Caroline's side on the roof of 929, and found her slumped and bleeding. Paramedics arrived shortly after police got to the scene, and they promptly began tending to her. As she was being taken out of the building, Caroline was very coherent, and she recounted the details of the attack to the officers accompanying her. "They responded wonderfully. They did everything that anyone could possibly do for that little girl. When they took her away, she was completely coherent. She was telling them everything," Williams recalled.

Caroline was transported to St. Luke's-Roosevelt Hospital Center at 113th Street and Amsterdam Avenue in a city Emergency Medical Service ambulance. She was wheeled into the emergency room at 2:05 a.m. on Sunday, December 2. She had nine stab wounds to her chest area, and was still coherent as the emergency room personnel worked to save her. She was scheduled for emergency surgery, and was taken into the operating room and anesthetized at 2:55 a.m. Unfortunately, Caroline died on the operating table at 7:30 a.m.

An autopsy was carried out, and the medical examiner's conclusions were released on December 3. The city's Chief Medical Examiner, Dr. Elliot Gross, stated that Caroline had died due to "multiple stab wounds with penetration of the left lung and liver." According to Dr. Gross, either the wound to the liver or the lung could have been fatal.

**Investigation**

Following Caroline's death, Assistant Chief Richard P. Dillon, who was in charge of detectives in Manhattan, held a news conference to speak about the case. He stated that Caroline had only offered a cursory description of the assailant, stating that he was "male black, light skinned, with an apparently clean- shaven face and a square jaw." He explained that she had not given any other details, especially pertaining to the man's height, approximate age or weight. "It is very little to go on, but it is still early in this case," he added. He stated that officers from the 24th precinct had gotten minimal information from Caroline while they were on the roof, but that questioning stopped because paramedics were administering oxygen to her. After she was brought into the emergency room, Dillon stated, a doctor told officers that her condition "was critical but stable and she was expected to survive." Two detectives who were put on the case decided to head to the crime scene first. They had been informed that the hospital's records stated that Caroline's life was not in imminent danger, so they believed they had enough time to get her statement later. However, when they arrived at the hospital at 3:15 a.m., Caroline was already in the operating room.

Dillon stated that police had been unable to recover the murder weapon, and had not found a witness who saw the assailant escape from the scene. He stated that the killer most likely first attacked Caroline in the elevator, but that they were unsure of the assailant's escape route. There were the eight flights of stairs at 929, as well as the fire escapes of the adjacent building. He added that there were no similar sex crimes or robberies in the neighborhood, and urged the public to reach out to police with any information. The deputy police commissioner for public information, Alice T. McGillion, revealed that a theater ticket stub and Playbill for the Saturday evening Broadway performance of "Hurlyburly" had been found in Caroline's handbag. McGillion stated that investigators were trying to determine where Caroline went to after the play, but that all signs made them believe that she had gone home alone. Later, she updated her statement, revealing that Caroline had gone for dinner at a restaurant. Police declined to reveal the name of the restaurant. McGillion also stated that the assailant had taken $12 from Caroline during the robbery, and that Caroline had spoken to the nurses and doctors at the hospital, mainly expressing regret as to why she didn't let the assailant have sex with her. "She indicated to us that he wanted to have sex and she resisted," McGillion said. Caroline reportedly said, "All this for $12. I should have given him the money. I should have let him do it. I should have given in."

Anne Burton, the hospital's spokesperson, was quick to speak out against some of the statements assistant chief Dillon made during the press conference. Burton maintained that "I have found nobody" who talked to police and gave them that particular medical appraisal, and that there was no one at the hospital who would have barred officers from talking to Caroline while she was in the emergency room. Burton stated that during those 50 minutes that Caroline was in the emergency room, doctors reports stated that "was in shock, but she was conscious and spoke coherently." She added that there were two officers who arrived at the hospital with Caroline, but none of them made a request to speak to her.

**Arrest**

On December 6, 1984, at 11 a.m., investigators arrived at the home of 21 year old Emmanuel Torres, at 49 West 225th Street in the Kingsbridge section of the Bronx, and arrested him for the murder of Caroline Rose Isenberg. Emmanuel had initially been interviewed by police on Sunday, December 2, at his Bronx apartment, as police worked to narrow down the field of suspects. The Chief of Detectives, Richard Nicastro, held a press conference following Emmanuel's arrest, and stated that there was little information to go on when the investigation began, but that it got easier when they narrowed their pool of suspects down to people who were familiar with the building itself. About 40 investigators were involved in the case, and Emmanuel was arrested the day after Caroline's burial in Boston – which was attended by over 1,000 people.

Chief Nicastro declined to reveal how Emmanuel became the prime suspect in the case, although he maintained that there was "diligent interviewing of witnesses, people in the area who gave information here and there." He stated that Emmanuel had two prior arrests – for assault and possession of a weapon in July of 1983 and fare beating 1982. According to Nicastro, Emmanuel had run back into the building and hidden in a locked room in the basement shortly after the stabbing. He stated that the officers who responded to the scene did not search the building at the time because they believed that the assailant couldn't possibly be in the building. However, after canvassing the scene and neighboring streets, detectives believed that the assailant may have hidden inside the building because "there were people on the street that night, and we could find no one who saw anyone flee." To bolster their theory that the assailant had been familiar with the building, investigators discovered that Emmanuel had lived at 929 West End Avenue until November 1983, when he moved to the Bronx apartment. At the time of the arrest, his father, Alex Torres, had been working as the building's superintendent for four years. According to Nicastro, Emmanuel had apparently gone to the building on the night of the murder "to do a rip-off."

Following his arrest at 11 a.m., Emmanuel was officially charged with second degree murder at 7:30 p.m. Just after 9 p.m., investigators led Emmanuel out of the 24th precinct and transported him in an unmarked police vehicle to Police Headquarters for booking. At the time, he was dressed in a plaid shirt, corduroy jacket, blue jeans, and brown work boots. As he made his way through the throng of reporters and photographers, he began shouting obscenities, and went as far as calling Caroline a "slut," among other derogatory names. He also added: "She deserved it. It was her fault." The following day, on December 7, the prosecutor assigned to Emmanuel's case, Assistant District Attorney in Manhattan Patrick J. Dugan, stated that Emmanuel had made a confession to police and that he gave "a detailed and graphic description of the murder." He also revealed that Emmanuel had bragged about the crime to at least one other person, who would be testifying for the prosecution when the trial commenced. Dugan also stated that additional evidence included the fact that Emmanuel had been "observed in the building where the crime took place shortly after the murder."

One police official stated that Emmanuel had offered an alibi, stating that he was at his mother's house in the Bronx on Saturday night and Sunday morning. However, investigators quickly called out the discrepancies in his statement, pointing out that various witnesses put him at a party on Saturday night in the Inwood section in Manhattan, and others saw him at 929 West End Avenue shortly after the murder. The official also revealed details of Emmanuel's confession that were riddled with discrepancies. Emmanuel told detectives that he had accosted Caroline in the building's hallway, and that she had initially agreed to have sex with him. However, she later changed her mind and began screaming for help, so he stabbed her nine times. This was disputed by Caroline's dying statement, as she had told an officer that the assailant had forced her to the rooftop at knife-point, and that he began stabbing her when she refused to have sex with him. The official also revealed that Emmanuel had led officers to the murder weapon following his confession – the folding knife with a four inch blade was recovered from an apartment belonging to one of Emmanuel's friends.

Emmanuel was arraigned in Manhattan Criminal Court on December 7, with Judge Allen G. Alpert presiding. Dugan maintained in court that "Our case is a strong one," and urged the judge not to grant Emmanuel bail. He described the defendant as "an aimless, irresponsible young man whose life style consisted of drinking beer and smoking dope." He added that Emmanuel was unemployed, had never held a job, and that he belonged to a divided family that "has no control over him." Dugan told the court that there was no reason to believe that Emmanuel would appear in court for his hearing if he was released on bail. Judge Alpert seemed to share the same sentiment, as he granted the prosecution's motion to deny Emmanuel bail.

Emmanuel, defended by a lawyer from the Legal Aid Society, Samuel R. Rosen, remained quiet throughout the arraignment hearing. He was not required to enter a plea of guilty or not guilty at the time, and Rosen made no request for bail for his client. He was transferred to the House of Detention for Men on Rikers Island, pending another hearing on December 12.

### Alfredo Torres' Interview

When word of Emmanuel's arrest made its way back to 929 West Avenue, residents of the building were more than willing to share their sentiments regarding the 21 year old. Many neighbors stated that Emmanuel had a history of bizarre behavior. Monique Blomquist, the 16-year-old daughter of Dian Blomquist, told *New York Daily News*: "He is not the kind of man you want to associate with. The whole thing has me hysterical. It could have been me." Noreen Williams stated that Emmanuel had killed her roommate's dog after he was asked to watch the animal. Tavares Toririo, another resident, stated that Emmanuel and his brother "stole carpets right out of my apartment." While Caroline's death was met with resounding sadness and grief, Emmanuel's arrest was no surprise.

Dr. Alfredo Torres, Emmanuel Torres' older brother, agreed to an interview with the New York Times following his brother's arrest, and hoped to explain how Emmanuel, the youngest of four brothers, ended up the way he was. At the time of the interview, 31-year-old Alfredo was a third year internal medicine resident in Rochester General Hospital. He graduated from the Fieldston School in the Riverdale section of the Bronx, Hobart College in Geneva, N.Y., and the University of Rochester Medical School. Speaking about his brother, Dr. Alfredo stated: "I have asked myself this question many times. I guess the only answer is I always had a goal. Ever since I can remember as a little boy, I told everybody I was going to grow up to be a doctor.

I was laughed at a lot by the other kids in school. They couldn't believe that a janitor's son would grow up to be a doctor. I stuck it out, did what I had to do and I got there."

Alfredo explained that Emmanuel's personality greatly changed following an accident that occurred when he was seven or eight. According to Alfredo, Emmanuel had just gotten off the school bus two blocks from their home on East 181st Street in the Bronx when he was hit by a car and the driver fled the scene. "He really was in fact affected by that accident. Following that, he more or less misbehaved an increasing amount and got in trouble in school. [He] became easily agitated at times - he was more likely to go away and be by himself."

Alfredo told the paper about his family, stating that their parents, Alex Torres and Neida Villanueva, immigrated to New York from San Juan, Puerto Rico, in the 1950s when he was an infant. They moved from one rundown building to another in the South and East Bronx. Their father, who was proficient with boilers, electrical wiring and plumbing, got work as a superintendent. They got three more sons, Edward, Angel, and Emmanuel. Alex and Neida separated when Alfredo was in junior high school, and the kids moved in with their mother. Neida was asthmatic, and she was prone to serious attacks, which rendered her unable to work. The divorce forced her to apply for disability. Emmanuel's fights in school, Alfredo explained, was a constant worry to their mother. She talked to Emmanuel's teachers on various occasions, and even sent him for a psychiatric evaluation one time.

He stated that the last time he had seen Emmanuel was in July 1983, and that Emmanuel had asked to move in with him in Rochester. Alfredo, a struggling resident, didn't think that Emmanuel, who was uneducated, would be able to easily find a job in Rochester. He planned on inviting Emmanuel to Rochester when his residency ended, but that was never to be. When asked about his brother's arrest records, Alfredo maintained that he had been unaware that Emmanuel had ever been arrested. He also stated that he was unaware Emmanuel's lifestyle involved smoking dope and drinking beer. He stated that he found out his brother had been arrested for murder when a newspaper reporter reached out to him. The news, he said, came as a shock and brought him to tears. He said, "I've never seen him do anything of a violent nature I've seen him pound a table when he's angry, but I've done that myself when I'm angry. He's a very outgoing person. He has the ability to make people like him. He likes to joke. He likes to laugh. I've seen him meet a total stranger and engage in a very nice conversation."

Speaking about his mother's reaction to the news, Alfredo said: "My mother was in tears. She's still a very severe asthmatic. She gets worse with any type of emotional stress. I'm worried what this might do to her physical health." He called his father to confirm whether he knew about Emmanuel's arrest: "He was crushed. The last thing he said to me was he never dreamed of anything like this happening."

**Conviction**

Before his trial began, Emmanuel's attorney, Lawrence Levner, filed a motion seeking to suppress Emmanuel's confession as well as the media's videotapes in which Emmanuel called Caroline a "slut" and shouted that "it was her fault." Levner Supreme Court Justice Stephen V. Crane to suppress the confession on the grounds that "police beat it out of Torres, and that they knew he had an unresolved assault case in the Bronx but refused to call his lawyer." On May 27, 1985, Torres told the court that he only signed the confession because "I was scared out of my wits" and "I thought I was going to die." He claimed that he sustained at least 35 blows to his body, courtesy of police, and that they threatened to kill him if he didn't confess. Levner also told the court that police had colluded with the press to get Emmanuel to say something "dramatic and incriminating for television cameras." Emmanuel claimed that officers had also coached him on what to say when he was in front of the cameras. However, Justice Crane ruled that both the confession and videotapes were admissible because "These accusations do not comport with the demeanor of the witnesses who allegedly participated in the beatings," and that there was nothing about the police officers who testified to "remotely suggest they forced him to repudiate his Sixth Amendment rights." Crane also pointed out that as Emmanuel walked out of the 24th precinct without a limp – the videotapes showed – despite claimed that he was hit repeatedly on his knee caps with a pistol butt, and there were no signs of the blows he allegedly received.

Following 13-day trial, the jury, composed of eight men and four women, returned with a verdict on Friday, June 28, 1985 after six and a half hours of deliberation over the course of two days. As jury foreman John Costello announced the verdict on the four counts of murder – murder during a robbery, murder during a rape attempt, murder during a sexual assault and intentional murder – Emmanuel swayed slightly. Following the verdict, Justice Crane ordered the Emmanuel Torres undergo a psychiatric evaluation, and set the sentencing trial for August 5, 1985. Emmanuel responded by shouting "I don't need no shrink," and banged on the defense table before pushing back his chair violently. He was led out of the court shouting.

On August 5, Justice Crane sentenced Emmanuel, whom he referred to as Manny, to serve 25 years to life for the murder of Caroline Rose Isenberg. Justice Crane stated that the crime was of "Shakespearean proportions in its foul and tragic dimensions." He added: "To this day, you have never expressed regret at the murder of this beautiful human being. All you have ever done is boast about it to police, to television reporters and to fellow inmates."

In response, Emmanuel, wearing dungarees and a T-shirt, pounded his chest and said: "In my heart, I have lost everything. I have lost respect. I have lost my self-respect. I have lost my hope. I have lost my life. I stand before you in this court, and I look above your head to the words 'In God We Trust,' and I do trust God. It's man I can't trust."

However, Justice Crane maintained that Emmanuel was, without a doubt, guilty of the crime.

# LISA MONTGOMERY

Lisa Montgomery would meet Bobbie Joe Stinnett in an on-line chatroom called "Ratter Chatter" under the pretext that she wanted to purchase a rat terrier puppy from her.

But what she really wanted from the pregnant Bobbie Joe was her baby.

Lisa would arrive at the Stinnett home and strangle the young woman into unconscious before cutting out the baby from her stomach with a kitchen knife.

She would then show case the baby around her small town, introducing her as "Abigail."

Investigative authorities would find out that Lisa would suffer from what psychiatrists called "pseudocyemesis." A psychological delusion where the subject believes she is pregnant.

The gruesome crime would shock the town of Skidmore, Missouri with its population of only 300 people. Once a community where they could keep their doors unlocked at night, the townsfolk would never be the same.

## BOBBIE JOE STINNETT

Bobbie Joe had lived in the small town of Skidmore, Missouri all of her life. She was a shy but happy cheerleader in high school and graduated with honors of May of 2000.

"She was intelligent and fun-loving," Bobbie Jo's mother Becky Harper said. "She never knew a stranger."

Three years after graduating, Bobbi Joe would marry her childhood sweetheart in Zeb Stinnett. The couple would tie the knot on April 26th, 2003.

"She was real quiet," Zeb said. "She pretty well kept to herself. I was the same way. I guess that's why we clicked so well."

Bobbie Joe would work at the Earl May Garden Center which served as both a pet store and plant nursery. Zeb worked in production at Kawasaki manufacturing. Later, Bobbie Joe would join Zeb at the plant and together they were saving money to buy their first home.

To make money on the side, Bobbie Joe was also a champion breeder of rat terriers. She ran the side business with her husband and they deemed the business "Happy Haven Farms.

"Our puppies are placed in only the very best homes with the family that fits them best," the website read. "Let us help you find your next pet, rat terrier or otherwise."

Bobbie Joe would also engage in on-line forums that discussed rat terriers. She would often be the go-to person to chat with because of her expertise in the genetics of breeding.

It was here in this on-line chat room she would meet "Darlene Fischer". Fischer was accused of misrepresenting her dog's pedigree by other members in the forum but Bobbie Jo would defend her.

Little did she know that Fischer was doing more than misrepresenting her dog's breed.

She was misrepresenting herself.

Darlene Fischer was really Lisa Montgomery.

"(Lisa) told us all she was pregnant with twins," chat room member Nancy Strudle said. "And about a month and a half ago her messages were 'I lost one of the twins. It's so terrible, but they saved one twin.' We didn't believe she was pregnant. I don't know how she fooled her family and community."

Bobbie Joe had met "Darlene" at a dog show in Abilene, Kansas in November of 2003. A few years later, "Darlene" would again touch base with Bobbie Joe via the Internet message boards of her rat terrier site.

"I was recommended to you," Lisa Montgomery wrote under her pseudonym. "And have been unable to reach you by either phone or email. Please get in touch with me soon as we are considering the purchase of one of your puppies and would like to ask you a few questions."

Bobbie Joe would e-mail Lisa back and the two would arrange a meeting.

Later that afternoon Bobbie Jo received a call from her mother, Becky. Her mother wanted her to come pick her up from her job at Sumy Oil. Bobbie Jo stated that she couldn't as she was waiting on a customer to come look at the puppies. At that moment, Lisa's red Toyota Corolla parked outside.

"There they are," Bobbie Jo said. "I've got to go."

It would be the last time they would ever speak.

LISA MONTGOMERY

Lisa Montgomery's life was troubled from the beginning. It was alleged that she was sexually abused by a stepfather as well as emotionally abused by her own mother.

John Patterson, Lisa's biological father, would express regret when he abandoned his daughters to their mother.

Lisa's mother, Judy Shaughnessy, wanted out of the marriage but John didn't fight for custody of the children as he was an alcoholic at the time.

"(I made a mistake) leaving my two daughters with that crazy lady."

Lisa's half-sister, Diane Mattingly, would agree with Patterson in that their mother was no angel.

"It was like walking on egg shells," Mattingly recalled. "You could never please her. If you did something wrong, you got hit."

"Lisa was raised in an abusive home," forensic psychiatrist Paula Orange said. "But she did not have any violent tendencies in her background. She was a well-versed liar and probably used this as a way of coping with an out of control, angry mother. So she developed a lot of negative coping mechanisms. This doesn't excuse her behavior but it does give us an idea of where she was coming from."

After Patterson left the family, Denise would be put up for adoption as their mother told them that it was their fault that he left.

"(Lisa) was clinging to me. I was her mother in reality," Mattingly said. "I was the one who protected them. I was the one who took care of them."

These early traumatic episodes would be the catalyst for the adult mental illnesses of Lisa. She would become obsessed with pregnancies and develop a lifelong habit of never telling the truth about anything.

Carl Boman, who was both the ex-husband and stepbrother of Lisa, would state that Montgomery saw pregnancy as a way to get attention. The couple would have three daughters and a son in less than four years. She would then get a tubal ligation without any forethought as doctors warned her against having more babies.

But Lisa would cheat on Carl during their tumultuous fourteen-year marriage. She would move from her native Oklahoma to New Mexico and then settle in Kansas.

"She was selfish," Boman said."A chronic liar with low self-esteem and critical of others. But she didn't have the potential for violence."

Lisa would pretend to be pregnant with Carl a few times during their marriage. Carl would file for divorce in 1993 but in 1994 they would reconcile and remarry. Why? Because Carl thought she was pregnant and didn't want to leave the baby abandoned.

Four years later, however, Lisa would file for divorce. She took their four children and moved in with Kevin Montgomery. Kevin had three kids of his own and they formed a "Brady Bunch" style union in his home of Melvern, Kansas.

Kevin was a quiet guy, an electrician by trade while Lisa was a housewife. She talked only of herself or her children, spending her days raising goats for wool. She would teach all of the children how to weave, dye and spin the yarn. But neighbors would describe all of the children as unkempt and dirty as when she wasn't weaving wool she was "vegging out on the couch."

Still, one of her older daughters remembers their time together fondly. Lisa would make old-fashioned dresses and bonnets with her daughters before they would attend fall festivals. She also encouraged one of her daughters to play football on the boy's team, going so far as addressing the school board to make it happen.

She would marry Kevin two years into their living arrangement as Lisa would claim to be pregnant. She began walking around the house in maternity clothes and announce a due date of December. She told everyone who would listen about her pregnancy, including Pastor Mike Wheatly.

The pastor told Lisa that she was "kind of small to be having a baby that soon."

"I've always had small babies," Lisa said, he didn't pursue the topic any further.

Kevin, who worked at a sign company over seventy miles away from their home, firmly believed that Lisa was pregnant.

"It was impossible for Lisa Montgomery to have another child," crime writer William Phelps said. "Her tubes were not tied. Her tubes were burned, cauterized. Which is an irreversible process. How could a husband sleep next to his wife of nine months and not know that she's pregnant? How could he look at her when she got out of the shower and not know he was pregnant? Didn't he go to any of the doctor's appointments? Lisa Montgomery manipulated this guy to believe that she was pregnant."

Meanwhile, former husband and step-brother Carl worried about his children under Lisa's care. He filed for sole custody which would force Lisa to admit in court that she was not pregnant. Carl knew Lisa's game. Once the judge saw Lisa's mental delusion first hand it would be easy for him to win custody.

Still, Lisa was adamant about playing the pregnancy card.

"She begins to buy diapers," Phelps said. "She begins to buy baby items. She tells the town, the husband, the children, everyone around her is pregnant. She lied through her childhood. Her teen years, her adult life. One of the lies she perpetrated was I'm pregnant. Lisa would say 'I'm pregnant, I'm pregnant, I'm pregnant' but then she would cover the lie with 'I miscarried.'"

"She begins to wear baggy clothes. She begins to make doctor's appointments. Fake doctors' appointments. She begins to swallow air when people are around. She begins to do all these things knowing that when the ninth month comes he's not going to have a baby."

This time, however, Lisa really needed a baby.

Lisa would go into grocery stores and shopping malls looking for a baby. She approached one woman holding an infant in a grocery store aisle.

"God, what a beautiful baby," Lisa said to the young mother.

"Thank you."

"I can hold her for you," Lisa offered. "You can do your shopping. She'll be safe with me."

The young woman was taken aback by Lisa's offer and overall demeanor. She politely excused herself and headed out of the store.

But Lisa still needed a baby.

"Lisa had a creepy vibe about her," Orange said. "She was more than awkward, she had a rat-like appearance with her hang-dog face and black-rimmed glasses. She would look down at the floor when she would talk to someone and gave off a vibe of an inbred Annie. Bobbie Joe, however, was not the judgmental type. So when the two met, Bobbie Joe wouldn't let any kind of street sense take over. She would want to be fair and non-judgmental."

Surfing around on the Internet, Lisa would visit her favorite on-line chatroom called "Ratter Chatter", a dog breeding forum dedicated to rat terriers.

Clicking through the pages, she sees pictures of Bobbie Joe and the puppies.

"The one thing she notices about Bobbie Joe," Phelps said. "Is that Bobbie Joe is pregnant."

"I think she looked at Bobbie Joe as being an incubator," Boman said.

Montgomery would use the pseudonym "Darlene Fischer" and wrote to Stinnett that she was pregnant also. Making every effort to befriend Bobbie Joe, the two women chatting via Instant Messenger and had conversations about their pregnancies. Montgomery then informed Stinnett that she wanted to buy a dog from her and arranged a meeting at her home.

"Lisa Montgomery is communicating with Bobbi Jo Stinnet online," Phelps said. "She's someone who enjoys these types of dogs that Bobbie Joe raises. Makes a date with Bobbie Joe to look at some puppies. But inside Lisa's car she has a knife, a rope, and a home birthing kit."

Thinking Lisa arrived at her home to look at the puppies, Bobbie Joe lets the woman inside without a second thought.

"Lisa Montgomery looks at the puppies," Phelps said. "She asks Bobbie Joe to bend down to pick up the puppy. She took out the rope, put it around her neck and choked her out."

Bobbie Joe did struggle with Lisa as some of her assailant's blonde hair was found in her fist, indicating that she had pulled out some of Montgomery's hair before she was subdued.

Lisa then cut the premature infant out of Bobbie Joe's stomach, slicing her open laterally with the kitchen knife.

"The evidence to me shows that she regained consciousness while the incision was being made, a struggle ensued and she was strangled again," Dr. Mary Case said. The 23-year old Bobbie Joe would fight desperately against the 39-year old Montgomery. But her attacker had the kitchen knife.

Lisa would slice across Bobbie Jo's body in a furious assault, cutting up her hands, face, and elbows. She would inflict eight jagged slices across Bobbie Jo's stomach.

Dr. Case believed that Bobbi Joe struggled upright because there was a large amount of blood found on the bottom of her feet. So she was either standing or sitting with her knees raised when Montgomery sliced her open. This could not have been possible had she been unconscious.

Lisa then removed the baby and cut the umbilical cord. Initially, it was thought that Bobbie Joe was murdered by someone who had someone medical skill.

"I think that maybe it's not as complicated as it might seem," Sheriff Graves said. "I'm not a medical expert, but I think anyone with a reasonable amount of skill could probably accomplish this."

Now with a newborn infant in her hands, Lisa could prove all of her doubters wrong.

She had a baby of her own.

Bobbie Joe would be found by her mother, Becky. She came into the Stinnett home and found her daughter laying in a pool of blood.

Becky would call 911.

"It looks like her stomach had exploded!" she said in her harrowing phone call.

"The images that are in your head are horrible," Boman said. "The idea of what happened. I mean it still effects me. I was allowed to see evidence and pictures and stuff and it's terrible."

Paramedic attempts at trying to revive Bobbie Joe would prove to be unsuccessful.

She was pronounced dead at St. Francis Hospital in Maryville, Missouri.

Lisa traveled along an isolated back road with her kidnapped baby. At some point, she either found a watering hole or stepped into a fast food restaurant to wash the baby down. She then

She then sealed her belly button with a pair of clips, giving herself the appearance of someone who just left the hospital. Lisa then called her husband Kevin. She told him she had gone shopping in Topeka, went into labor and had given birth.

Her husband was surprised but pleased by the news.

Her pastor, Mike Wheatly, was next on the call list. Lisa and her family had attended his church for the past four years. Wheatly was again, surprised at the revelation and stated that he looked forward to seeing the newborn.

Kevin and their high-school-age children then got into their car and drove to Topeka. They would meet Lisa in the parking lot of a Long John Silver's restaurant. They would show off "Abigail" in the restaurant to other customers.

Kevin, Lisa, and the stolen newborn would drove home in his pick-up. Their teenage children would drive home in Lisa's car, a red Toyota Corolla.

They brought the baby to see Pastor Mike Wheatly and he expressed surprise that there actually was a baby. "I was doubtful that she was pregnant in the first place," Wheatly said.

But both the pastor and his wife took turns holding Abigail for about an hour's visit. The church couple did,however, think it was odd that a newborn baby should be out doing the rounds so soon.

Police did not rule out anyone in the murder of Bobbie Joe Stinnett. Initially, they would question Zeb but the husband had an airtight alibi. He was at work.

They would issue an Amber Alert for the baby and could only hope that the infant was still alive.

Authorities would catch a break almost immediately, however. An alert dog breeder from North Carolina would inform the FBI of Stinnett's exchanges with "Darlene". She sent the links over to the FBI which read as follows:

"Darlene, I've emailed you with the directions so we can meet," Bobbie Jo wrote. " I do so hope that the email reaches you. Great chatting with you on messenger. And do look forward to chatting with you tomorrow a.m...talk to you soon Darlene!"

Computer investigators then contacted internet providers who were able to trace the fictitious e-mailer to Montgomery's home which was over 130 miles away.

Police then began surveillance of the home and spotted Lisa with the newborn baby. A "dirty, red pinkish, two door vehicle" was reported being seen outside Stinnett's home by a neighbor and the same vehicle matched that description outside Montgomery's home.

A dirty and dusty red Toyota Corolla.

Authorities would arrest Lisa and save the baby who was immediately taken to the hospital.

Lisa double-downed on her lies when interrogated by police. She told them she had delivered the baby herself only a day earlier. They checked with the Topeka women's clinic where Lisa claimed to have delivered Abigail only to find out that they had no babies born there on the day that Lisa claimed.

Lisa would then succumb to the pressure and confess to the killing and kidnapping.

"She confessed to having strangled Stinnett and removing the fetus," the local sheriff said. "Lisa Montgomery further admitted the baby she had was Stinnett's baby and that she had lied to her husband about giving birth to a child."

Bobbie Joe's baby would be brought to the Neonatal Intensive Care Unit at Topeka Hospital. Zeb would later describe his daughter as "a miracle."

The gruesome murder would stun the residents of Skidmore, Missouri. A small town with just over 300 people, things like that never happened there.

"It's very hard for me to accept this," Nodaway County Sheriff Ben Espey said. "Nobody here could ever perceive this taking place—to have a fetus taken out of someone's womb and then doing an Amber Alert to try to find a child."

. "We felt betrayed. We were angry," Pastor Mike Wheatly said. "But most of all, we're very, very, very sad."

The crime would resonate in the dog breeding community where Bobbie Jo Stinnett was so popular as well.

"I am sitting here in shock, not knowing how to break this," a user named Teresa wrote. "I just received a phone call from a reporter in Missouri saying that Bobbie was killed today and her fetus stolen! I am absolutely horrified!"

"I cannot believe how sorrowful I am," a chatroom user named Jill wrote. "They have taken Lisa into custody. I don't know what is worse—the horrible crime—or the possibility that it might be Lisa. Someone just shoot me."

Lisa would be charged with "kidnapping resulting in death." Her husband Kevin would not be charged as authorities believed that he knew nothing of Lisa's intent or act of murder.

"My heart ain't broke just for me and Lisa and her kids," Kevin Montgomery said. "It is them (the Stinnett family) too. That was a precious baby. I know."

During a pre-trial hearing, a neuropsychologist would state that the head injuries that Montgomery suffered a few years ago could have damaged a part of her brain which controls aggression. Her attorneys would also argue that Montgomery also suffered from pseudocyesis, a delusion that she was pregnant.

A second neuroscientist would dovetail this assertion, stating that Montgomery's childhood sexual abuse and post-traumatic stress disorder made her susceptible to pseudocyesis.

Prosecuting attorney Roseann Ketchmark dismissed the theories, however, calling them "voodoo science."

Famed forensic psychiatrist Park Dietz would testify for the prosecution. He had been the expert psychiatrist for other high-profile cases such as Jeffrey Dahmer, the Unabomber, Andrea Yates and Susan Smith.

Dietz would testify that Montgomery did not suffer from pseudocyesis and discounted the theory as "outrageous."

Jurors found Montgomery's excuses "outrageous" and would find her guilty of murder on October 22nd, 2007. She was given a death sentence and in April 2008 a judge upheld the decision.

Her case US Supreme Court who denied Montgomery's petition to be removed from death row.

Lisa Montgomery is now being held at Federal Medical Center, Carswell in Fort Worth, Texas.

She is in line to become the third woman to be put to death by the federal government since 1927 and the first in over fifty years.

Lisa's oldest daughter would move in with friends while her youngest child would move out of state. The two middle children would live with her ex-husband and step-brother, Carl.

At Bobbie Jo's funeral, her husband Zeb would read the 23rd Psalm beside her casket. The Reverend Herald Hamon of Skidmore Christian Church, the same man who married Bobbie Jo and Zeb, would deliver her eulogy.

Bobbie Jo would be the third member of her family to have been murdered in the early 2000s. She had a cousin that was stomped to death by her boyfriend as well as having another cousin who disappeared.

"Abigail" has been renamed and lives with her father.

# BLACK WIDOW TILLIE KLIMEK

CARA DAVIDSON

Ottilie "Tillie" Klimek—born Ottilie Gburek—was a Polish American serial killer who was active in Chicago during the early 1900s. She allegedly murdered between six and 20 individuals by poisoning them with arsenic. Additional victims included her other husbands, a boyfriend, relatives and various neighbors with help of her cousin Nellie Koulik.

Klimek is purported to have experienced precognitive dreams which predicted her victims' actual dates of deaths; however, in reality, she was simply "scheduling" them as there is no historic evidence in any of the literature that she had any psychic gifts or precognition skills. While Klimek was arrested after nearly poisoning her last husband Joseph Klimek—for which she was tried, convicted, and given a life sentence—she was only convicted of one murder; that of her third husband, Frank Kupszcyk. She was sentenced to life in prison in 1923 and subsequently died on 20 November 1936.

### Early Life

Ottilie "Tillie" Klimek was born Ottilie Gburek in 1876 in Poland. When she was about a year old, her parents immigrated with her to the United States along with many eastern European lower classes who were among the first immigrants who left their homelands in search of a better life in the United States. The Gbureks settled in the north side Chicago neighborhood dubbed "Little Poland." At the time, Chicago boasted the second-largest Polish population in the world, after Warsaw, Poland. The families who settled in Little Poland were largely law-abiding and God-fearing people so when word of Klimek's later activities became known even her own people looked at her with disdain.

While there is scant information on much of Klimek's early life until her teenage years when she first married, there is ample evidence in the literature that she was an amazing cook. In fact, her special "stew" was her claim to fame, in more ways than one. Another of Klimek's special "gifts" was her self-proclaimed psychic ability that enabled her to accurately "predict" the deaths of certain people and animals. She began by predicting the demise of neighborhood pets which were almost always accurate. She then "predicted" the death of all of her husbands, a boyfriend, several relatives with whom she had quarreled or who had otherwise done her wrong.

Absent other early biological data, it is known that Klimek married her first husband, John Mitkiewicz, in 1890, when she was just 14 years of age. He died in 1914 after a relatively short illness and his death certificate states that he died from a heart attack.

Shortly after collecting her life insurance check from her husband's death, Klimek married Joseph Ruskowski, whom she had met through a matchmaker. He would pass away a mere three months later and Tillie was on the lookout for another relationship.

This time the unlucky fellow was Joseph Guszkowski who is listed as a boyfriend who allegedly jilted her; however, in some accounts he is listed as one of Klimek's husbands, so the legal nature of their relationship is not conclusive. Guszkowski would die in 1914 as well. At his funeral Klimek acted wholly surprised that she had such bad luck with men and also cursed her "ominous dreams" in front of everyone. Whether her melodramatic display actually convinced others that she truly felt cursed and tragic is up for speculation.

Klimek then her wed third husband, Frank Kupszcyk. The unhappily-married couple lived in an apartment at 924 N. Winchester; the same apartment in which she had resided with Joseph Guszkowski.

On 25 April 1921, a mere two years after they exchanged their vows, Frank died shortly after Klimek "foretold" his death from one of her premonitions and within a year—in true grieving-widow form—Klimek was in another relationship.

Over the warnings and protestations of his family and friends, Joseph Klimek—who had attended Frank's funeral for some reason not fully explained in the literature except, perhaps, to get close to the newly-single Klimek—decided to marry the widow with the troubling reputation. The couple wed in 1921 and resided at 1453 Tell Place (later renamed Thomas Street). When Joseph became sick, the doctors suspected arsenic poisoning and subsequent medical tests confirmed their suspicions. Thankfully, Joseph survived and his wife was arrested for attempted murder. The full extent of her murderous ways would soon be made public.

## The Crimes

Klimek was frequently seen as a psychic by her neighbors and others in Chicago as her "uncanny talent" of foreseeing the exact dates of deaths for her five husbands—only four actually perished at her hand—as well as other neighbors was seen as both astounding and a little bit alarming because nobody wanted to know when they were supposed to die.

Klimek's "talent", however, would soon be revealed as bogus, she knew damn well when these people would die because she would be the one to kill them. Her murderous spree began in 1914 and ended in 1922 when she was arrested for the attempted murder of her last husband Joseph Klimek.

Called a "Black Widow", Klimek started down this macabre road rather late in life when compared to other well-known black widows. She was in her mid-30's when she claimed her first victim—her first husband. Experts alleged that this is an age at which most husband-killing women stop their activities.

### *John Mitkiewicz*

In January 1914, Klimek "predicted" the death of her long-time husband, John Mitkiewicz, whom she had married in 1890. Klimek allegedly told a friend that she dreamt that she had discovered his corpse on a specific date a few weeks in the future and, of course, acted worried about the "news." When John fell sick on that exact day and died later that night, her friend was awestruck.

Klimek to have sprinted to the insurance office to collect the $1,000 proceeds upon his death. Eyebrows were not raised at this time because, after all, people died, wives inherited life insurance monies, and, ultimately, life went on.

But post-exhumation investigation would reveal that John had been poisoned with a lethal amount of arsenic.

Many assert that this first murder was one of convenience and profit that quickly became a way for Klimek to make a living by collecting life insurance payments and exact revenge on those she believed had wronged her.

### John Ruskowski

Klimek did not remain a widow for long. A mere two months later, she married John Ruskowski, a laborer who quickly became the subject of one of Klimek's precognitive dreams. Whereas neighbors—and John himself—initially laughed at her predictions and chalked them up to nonsense, when he died on the stated date in May 1914, they became true believers.

Klimek received approximately $1,200 in cash and just over $700 in life insurance funds from his death. Again, his death did not elicit much cause for alarm at the time.

### Joseph Guszkowski

Her next victim would be Joseph Guszkowski, whose relationship with Klimek differs depending upon the account one reads. In most reports, Joseph is listed as a boyfriend who allegedly jilted Klimek which, in turn, spurred her into action; while in other accounts John is stated to have been her fourth husband. Regardless of the actual relationship, the outcome did not change.

Klimek told Joseph—albeit in a roundabout way—that her previous husbands did not, exactly, perish from natural causes but that she had deliberately poisoned them with arsenic.

Scared shitless, Joseph sought to end their relationship. Klimek then threatened to bring Joseph to justice under the Mann Act; a piece of 1920s legislation that initially sought to stop interstate commerce of women for the purpose of sexual activity. Joseph became angrier and threatened to tell authorities about Klimek's "arsenic tendencies." This proved to be a very bad move when Klimek "foretold" his death which, not surprisingly, reached fruition exactly when she said it would.

### Frank Kupszcyk

Klimek married third husband Frank Kupszcyk in 1919 and he grew ill after consuming his wife's delicious vegetable soup with the one extra ingredient: arsenic. As Frank got sicker and sicker, Klimek would say things to her neighbors that her current husband "would not live long" and that he only had "two inches to live." She even taunted Frank to his face by telling him, "It won't be long now," and "You'll be dying soon."

Klimek sewed her own mourning hat—which she later wore at his funeral and at her trial—while sitting beside her husband as he was suffering on his deathbed. Klimek also had the audacity to ask her landlady for permission to store a coffin in the building's basement that she had purchased on sale for $30.

Frank eventually died in 1921. Klimek played loud and cheerful dance music on a phonograph in the same room and celebrated upon his death. At his service, Klimek reached into her dead husband's coffin to grab his ear and shouted, "You devil, you won't get up anymore!"

Klimek was listed as the sole beneficiary on her late husband's life insurance policy, and ultimately collected $675 from it.

It was during this time that Klimek was gaining notoriety with many wondering how she was able to attract husbands given the ominous ends of those who came before. Also, by this point, others in the community had started avoiding Klimek in public so as not to hear predictions about their own deaths.

### Joseph Klimek

Klimek's last husband Joseph Klimek—who married the black widow in 1921 even after being warned by friends and families—also became ill after they had been married for a short time. Klimek had spoken to her cousin Nellie Sturmer Koulik—who also "had a dead husband under her belt"—and confided in her that her latest marriage was not all rosy and that she was, in fact, sick and tired of her husband. When Nellie suggested divorce, Klimek said, "I will get rid of him some other way" to which Nellie allegedly gave her cousin a knowing look and a "goodly portion" of rat poison called "Rough on Rats" that was comprised of arsenic and easy to purchase at that time. Ironically, the slogan for the poison was "Don't die in the house."

Naturally, Joseph fell ill with some of the classic symptoms of arsenic poisoning: stiff legs and garlic-smelling breath.

Joseph's brother John became quite suspicious at his brother's rapid-onset illness and the fact that his sister-in-law didn't seem too worried. Compounding the problem was that two of Joseph's pet dogs had also recently died abruptly and under strange circumstances. John phoned his own doctor to come to the Klimek's residence to examine Joseph and the family physician immediately suspected that the sick man was suffering from arsenic poisoning. They took Joseph to the hospital and saved his life. After running several tests, this diagnosis was later confirmed.

While Joseph survived, he did have to spend a grueling three months in the hospital recuperating.

Klimek was subsequently arrested on 26 October 1922, for the attempted murder of her husband Joseph. She told the arresting officer that, "The next one I want to cook a dinner for is you. You made all my trouble."

### Other Victims

One of Klimek's cousins, Rose Chudzinski, became suspicious of Klimek's psychic "gift" and the tragic ends which befell her men she married. After Klimek had heard the rumors Rose had been spreading, the women quarreled; after which Klimek "predicted" Rose's death. Of course, Rose died in 1919, shortly after this argument which allegedly occurred at the Klimeks' wedding party.

Klimek's and Nellie's other victims include more cousins: 16-year-old Stanley Zakrzewski who died in 1912, 23-year-old cousin Stelle Zakrzewski who died in 1913, and 15-year-old Helen Zakrzewski who died in 1915. Ironically, when her cousins were ill, Klimek had been their primary caretaker and before their deaths, Klimek had allegedly reported she had precognitive dreams in which the cousins were all victims of some sort of deadly plague.

Nellie's infant daughter Sophie Sturmer died in 1917 and her twin brother Ben died one month later. Additionally, Nellie's first husband Wojek Sturmer died in 1918, and arsenic was found in his system after exhumation. Nellie's granddaughter Dorothy Spera died at the tragic age of two. Another of Nellie's sons, John Sturmer, fell ill after his father's death. He recovered; however, convinced that his mother poisoned him as well. Another of Nellie's daughters, Lillian Sturmer, lived at Klimek's house for about a year when she was 13. Although Lillian became deathly ill after eating Klimek's cooking she also survived but suffered serious heart trouble for the rest of her life.

A former boyfriend or sweetheart—or possibly another husband—named "Meyers" went missing in March 1923. Two of Klimek's neighbors—Rose Splitt and Stelle Grantowski—reportedly died after she gave them poisoned candy following an argument they had with Klimek.

Other victims survived. Cousin Nick Micko recovered from his arsenic poisoning after eating one of Klimek's delicious meals, and Bessie Kupszcyk—Klimek's husband Frank's sister-in-law—also fell ill after eating at Klimek's and she, too, recovered.

A neighborhood dog Klimek thought a nuisance who lived on Winchester Street when she had had also perished mysteriously, as had Joseph Klimek's two pet dogs.

In sum, there were 20 suspected victims, 12 of whom had died, seven who were still alive, and one who was missing.

**Investigation and Arrest**

The year-long investigation yielded much evidence. In addition to a multitude of macabre exhumations, there were also anonymous letters which referenced potential victims and poisoned candy.

It soon became evident that Joseph Klimek's illness was neither mysterious nor isolated. After Klimek's arrest, police received an anonymous letter which led to authorities' exhuming Frank Kupszcyk's body and, voila, the body was chock full of enough arsenic to kill a dozen men. As there was no arsenic in the surrounding soil, investigators had no other conclusion to draw than Frank was poisoned to death.

As would be expected in 1920's Chicago, local newspapers and tabloids had a field day with this information, as well as news that would soon break about additional exhumations.

Another anonymous letter named Klimek's cousin Nellie Koulik as another potential suspect and urged police to look more closely at her. The letter also insisted that police ought to exhume Nellie's first husband—Wojek Strummer—who died in 1918, and to check his body for lethal concentrations of arsenic as the cause of his death. Lo and behold, his body also contained fatal amounts of arsenic. Letters also indicted the two women as aiding and abetting each other's efforts in getting rid of other friends and relatives who had died under similarly mysterious circumstances.

Consequently, Nellie was arrested one week after Klimek.

At some point, police took Klimek to visit her husband in the hospital. Understandably, he was angry, upset, curious, and, thus, full of questions; however, she often replied with "I don't know" or admonished her husband to not bother her anymore about such trivial matters. It is reported that at one point Klimek overhead him asking a nurse for some water to which she replied that if he continued to be a troublemaker to just hit him over the head with a two-by-four. Before leaving, Klimek kissed her husband, said action baffling everyone given her demeanor toward him as well as the curious statements she had made to hospital staff.

While preparations were being made to exhume Klimek's first couple of husbands, two of her cousins arrived and requested that police exhume four additional bodies; those of three siblings who died under mysterious conditions after having eaten at Klimek's house and that Klimek had been angry with their mother, not to mention that she had had her precognitive dreams about them, as well as another cousin with whom Klimek had argued.

Police also learned about Joseph Guszkowski—Klimek's former boyfriend/husband—who also died under mysterious circumstances. Thus, additional exhumation orders were ordered and processed and both Klimek and Nellie were formally charged with murder: Klimek for Frank Kupszcyk, and Nellie for her first husband Wojek Strummer. However, after following the all of the clues and trails from the anonymous letters and other involved parties' recommendations, detectives found three more graves; very small ones belonging to Nellie's twin babies and her granddaughter.

Nellie had given birth to her twins—Sophie and Ben Sturmer—while still married to Wojek; however, as she was having an affair with her future second husband, Albert Koulik, at the same time, Wojek denied that he was the twins' biological father. Of course, Nellie did not take this refusal very well. Consequently, one twin, Sophie, died at eight months of age and the other, Ben, a month later. The third dead child was Nellie's two-year-old granddaughter, Dorothy Spera, who she also poisoned because Nellie's daughter (the child's mother) was critical of the way Nellie lived and the choices she had made. When the poor child fell ill, Nellie insisted on caring for her. Subsequently, the baby's feet and face swelled from the abundance of arsenic in her body and she eventually died in her grandmother's care.

Additional victims included other relatives, friends, and neighbors who had all eaten at Klimek's or Nellie's at some point and had fallen ill shortly thereafter.

Nellie's sister Cornelia was also arrested because Cornelia's son-in-law suspected that she was poisoning him by lacing his moonshine with arsenic.

Word got out that Klimek was likely not a singular serial killer but some sort of "high priestess of a Bluebeard clique" within the Little Poland, Chicago neighborhood. Assistant State Attorney W.F. McLaughlin had it in for Klimek from the get-go and made no bones about it. Many have suggested that he sought some sort of professional immortality he believed he could achieve through this case. Thus, he demonstrated considerable melodrama and exaggeration when he referred to the alleged Bluebeard clique as "the most astounding wholesale poisoning plot ever uncovered" as well as "the most amazing death plot in recent criminal history." This widespread accusation caused other neighborhood women to be arrested; however, they were subsequently released when the whole concept of such as clique was dispelled.

As for Klimek, however, McLaughlin wanted blood and vehemently sought the death penalty.

While in custody, Nellie's English-speaking capacity diminished considerably. She was also reported as being relatively happy and good natured given the situation—even allowing reporters to photograph her once she had fixed her hair, of course; however, she did have a reputation for hysterics, particularly in response to her cousin's poor choice and timing of various gallows humor. Oftentimes Klimek would convince Nellie that the authorities were on their way and that she was to be hanged and the naïve Nellie often believed her cousin's statements.

Conversely, Klimek, while in custody, was insolent, quiet, controlled, and icy—almost robot-like in her demeanor and lack of emotion. The only reactions she ever displayed was when she repeatedly—and vehemently—denied killing anyone. She was also rather emotional when she claimed that everyone was "picking on" and "making eyes" at her.

Despite her denials, there was ample physical evidence and Klimek's protestations of innocence were not believed by anyone, especially her husband Joseph.

**Trial**

The trial commenced on 27 February 1923, against the woman known as "Mrs. Bluebeard" and "The Polish Borgia"; the latter in reference to the infamous Borgia family of 15th- and 16th-century Spain whose members were noted for several heinous crimes including murder by arsenic poisoning.

Joseph Klimek was to be McLaughlin's star witness in the proceedings against his wife, the alleged leader of some heinous Bluebeard clique and poisoner of 20 people, in a trial in which State Attorney McLaughlin was enthusiastically seeking the death penalty. If successful, such would set a new precedent as the state of Illinois had never executed a woman and this is likely why McLaughlin was so passionate about finding Klimek guilty. So passionate, in fact, that he beseeched the jury throughout the entire proceedings to step it up and finally sentence a woman to death. And Klimek was his perfect woman—a husband-killer four times over.

Medical experts testified that Joseph experienced acute paralysis by the covert, prolonged, and regular introduction of arsenic into his food. As a result, he had lost the use of his legs due to the paralytic property of arsenic.

Joseph testified that after his wife talked him into purchasing more life insurance, her meals began to taste a bit "queer" but he never in a million years suspected that she was slowly killing him.

Klimek, in her own behalf, was adamant that she did not murder her husbands. She claimed that Frank died from alcohol poisoning;

saying this while wearing the death hat she had sewn while he lay dying. She also insisted that she loved her husbands deeply and they loved her as well. She also questioned the fuss made over the fact that people die all the time. However, by the end of the trial—and listening to the medical examiner's testimony that arsenic was, indeed, found in all of her husband's systems—her stoic façade had begun to crumble and, for the first time, Tillie Klimek looked somewhat anxious.

During the trial, psychiatrists testified about evaluations they had conducted while the women were awaiting trial. In their analyses, they alleged that both women had some type of mental defect and likely suffered from dementia praecox; a chronic and deteriorating psychotic disorder that causes rapid cognitive disintegration and that typically manifests itself in late adolescence or young adulthood. The women had also been assessed as having the intelligence of an 11-year-old child. This particularly interested the presiding judge because he knew that one of Nellie's sons had already been declared to be feeble-minded several years ago and the judge was a firm believer in genetics and an advocate of eugenics. Thus, he was of the mindset that if individuals were determined to be mentally inferior and prone to criminality then fieldworkers and police officers could keep their eyes on their relatives as they, in his mind, had a greater propensity for deviance as well. Such as mindset is a scary thing as history is rife with individuals with similar ideas who have committed horrible atrocities on those determined to be "lesser" people.

One critic of the psychological reports and tests asserts that because neither Klimek nor Nellie spoke perfect English that there was a great likelihood that they did not understand some of the questions or other aspects of the evaluation and this could have accounted for the results. Thus, had they been evaluated in their native language—or even had a translator provided—then, perhaps, the results would have been different because Klimek demonstrated, on many occasions, that she was extremely smart and cunning.

The trial was covered by many of the new wave of Chicago's "girl reporters" including Genevieve Forbes who was one of the country's pioneers with respect to females working the crime beat news. During that era, a female crime reporter was an anomaly. Genevieve interviewed Joseph in the hospital, she contacted Klimek's troubled parents, and she even tried to interview the stoic Klimek herself who Genevieve could not get to lower her guard even a tiny bit. Genevieve's analyses were oftentimes brutal and unforgiving but she also had a reputation for being relatively fair. Thus, her recognition that Klimek was, indeed, a vengeful, cunning, and dangerous woman rang true; as did her assessment that Nellie really posed little threat.

The public's perception of Klimek did not help matters much. Genevieve described the murderess as "a fat, squat Polish peasant woman", looking considerably older than her 40-something years, with "a lumpy figure, capacious hands and feet", and dull hair pulled back into a severe bun at the back of her head. Yet, despite the brutally honest and unflattering description, Genevieve did acknowledge Klimek's intelligence and dispelled aspects of the psychiatric testimony. Genevieve also wrote that because Klimek was neither beautiful nor "flawlessly American" she could not escape the widespread belief that she was stupid or slow or—as immigrants were commonly known at that time—a lowly peasant.

Other "journalists" reported that, unlike other women who killed their husbands and had been acquitted (think Kander and Ebb's epic play *Chicago* set during this era), Klimek, as mentioned, was neither beautiful nor charming. She also spoke poor English despite having lived in Chicago for pretty much her entire life. In other words, Klimek did not abide the established "rules" of the 1920's Chicago husband-murdering "game" which necessitated flirting, getting all dolled up, and sobbing demurely to elicit jury and judge favor or sympathy culminating in an acquittal. Thus, her trial evolved into a circus of sorts with the judge having to—on many occasions—threaten the courtroom with, "This is not a theater!"

While denying her responsibility, overtly denouncing her special psychic gift, and attempts to elicit sympathy and compassion for her bad luck with the men in her life, Klimek was confident that she would not be executed. In fact, she was correct. While the state did not have to enforce the death penalty as she was sentenced to life in prison without parole, the state did keep its promise to keep her locked up for the rest of her life.

Her trial concluded in March when she was found guilty of Frank's murder and she was sentenced to life in prison. At the time this was the harshest sentence ever given to a female defendant in the history of Cook County.

One interesting but understandable stipulation of her sentence was that she never be permitted to cook for the other inmates.

Whereas the public was initially interested in Klimek even though she wasn't as young and attractive as other murderesses over which the public would fawn, the public quickly lost interest in Chicago's latest husband killer. At the time, a female murderer was noteworthy; however, absent an equally noteworthy backstory—or stunning beauty—the once spectacular headline simply vanished from the public's consciousness.

Cousin Nellie's tedious year in prison alongside her unrepentant cousin culminated in her acquittal. Even though her own children had testified against her, the jury found her not guilty of giving Klimek the rat poison which killed Frank. After the acquittal, McLaughlin dropped the murder charge—even though her husband's body showed a high level of arsenic—against her for several reasons. First, with Klimek convicted and sentenced to life in prison, the whole idea of the Bluebeard clique lost its appeal. Secondly, other murderesses were taking over the front page and, as a result, the public's consciousness.

Klimek died in prison on 20 November 1936. Reports cite a heart attack as her cause of death.

**Aftermath**

Much reference is made to Klimek's use of poison throughout her murder spree. Poison is a common method for murder for women, according to several experts. This is likely because it enables killers to get close to their victims while also deciding when and how they would ultimately die. Further, poisoning was a relatively easy murder weapon throughout early history as the forensic knowledge and testing capabilities prevalent today were not as widely known or used. It was only when doctors presumed that Joseph Klimek had been poisoned that they specifically looked for evidence; thus finding arsenic in his system.

Additionally, the criminological literature is rife with theories about female offenders. Elizabeth Yardley and David Wilson, in their book *Female Serial Killers in Social Context* (2015), discuss the multiple motivations of female serial killers. For women, these motivations are largely profit or revenge. Klimek profited from three of her husband's deaths in terms of cashing in their life insurance policies, thus meeting the requirements to be classified as a "Black Widow." Another victim met his demise after allegedly breaking off their relationship so she sought revenge out of anger. The anger-vengeance motive arose again when she killed three of her cousins after having a disagreement with the victims' mother. Revenge was also cited in the death of her cousin Rose Chudzinski as Klimek poisoned Rose's dinner after the two women had an argument. Unlike male serial killers, females typically have multiple motives for their actions and such was, indeed, the case with Tillie Klimek.

Many have written that had Klimek been attractive and demure and everything the public wanted her to be then she would likely have been acquitted even though there was no doubt of her guilt. In fact, at the time, 28 women had been acquitted of murder and, of course, all 28 were attractive. Four others had been found guilty and these four were not attractive. Genevieve Forbes, in a follow-up, retrospective piece on Klimek wrote that she went to prison "because she had never gone to a beauty parlor." Regardless, Klimek adapted well to prison, even reportedly commenting on the delicious prison food.

Joseph Klimek died a few years after the trial. Whereas the cause of death was blamed on tonsillitis, at his autopsy it was discovered that his body was full of arsenic.

Tillie Klimek remains the most prolific female serial killer in Chicago history.

# THE MURDER OF JEFF WRIGHT

NATALIE HARRIS

The murder of Jeff Wright was one of the most brutal and controversial in Texas history. His wife, Susan Wright, stabbed him in excess of 193 times before burying his body in a shallow grave in the back of their home. What followed was a media frenzy as Susan was dubbed as the "Blue Eyed Butcher." Court TV televised the entire trial while numerous media outlets devoted special segments to the case.

But the picture didn't fit.

Susan was depicted as this cold-blooded, sadistic killer. Everyone who has met her, however, has come away feeling that she was a shy, polite woman who could not harm a fly. The prosecuting attorney would claim that her politeness was just an act...Was it an act? Or did Susan simply snap after being abused one time too many?

EARLY LIFE

There were three of the children altogether, Susan, Cindy and a brother named Jim. They were raised in an upper-middle-class home in Harris County. Susan's mother was a stay at home mom while her father was a mechanical engineer.

A shy and reserved child, Susan stated that she walked on eggshells at home as her father would abuse her mother.

"She was trained to put on a smile and make everything seem like it was all right," forensic psychologist Paula Orange said. "It became normal for her to see a father yelling at her mother and she thought it was something that went on in every household."

Susan's sister, Cindy, would maintain that Susan would have trouble standing up for herself. She tried out for the drill team and was berated by one of the older girls. Susan felt so violated that she transferred to another school.

Susan was a mediocre student in high school and made C's in the majority of her classes. She didn't date much but tried to get attention from boys. She had one boyfriend tell her she was "too fat" which prompted Susan to lose almost twenty pounds. At the age of eighteen, she had a boyfriend that told her to work as a topless dancer at a strip club called the Gold Cup.

She worked as a stripper there for about two months but grew tired of it, stating that the money wasn't worth it and that she did it to feel better about herself.

Susan then used the money to go a local community college where she enrolled in a nursing program. Still needing extra cash, she found began working as a hair stylist. She dropped out the nursing program just as fast as she quit exotic dancing, stating that the curriculum was too time-consuming and would cost too much.

"There are two ways to look at Susan's early life," Orange said. "One is to say that she was into the cocaine and fast lifestyle that the stripper scene would provide. The other is to say that perhaps she was looking for acceptance. Being a topless dancer is going to be judged harshly by adults. But to the young men she was trying to get attention from, it would be seen as something pretty cool."

Jeff Wright would see that something "pretty cool" in Susan the moment he laid eyes on her at a get together on Galveston Beach in Texas.

THE HANDSOME SUITOR

Jeff had been a notorious party animal in school. He enjoyed booze and cocaine but began thinking more about settling down as he turned thirty.

He then met the twenty-one-year-old Susan at the beach. She was a struggling waitress, he was a successful carpet and tile salesman. Smitten by her pretty face and blonde hair, he began pursuing her with vigor, showering Susan with expensive gifts and fancy dinners.

After a few months of dating, Susan announced that she was pregnant. Jeff would tell her that it would be "okay" if she got an abortion but they decided to keep the baby and marry instead. Susan, however, was upset that Jeff waited until she was eight months pregnant to propose.

A week after his proposal, the young couple exchanged vows in a small ceremony near Houston, Texas.

Susan would later claim that Jeffrey would change dramatically after the wedding night. He would taunt Susan, calling her a "fat ass" as she gained weight during the pregnancy. Susan became depressed after the baby was born and Jeff mocked her even further for seeing a doctor who diagnosed her with postpartum depression.

Jeff's controlling behavior got worse with time. He disallowed Susan to take the anti-depressants the doctor had prescribed her. He then began limiting the people she could have in her life, allowing Susan to see her mother but she could only be out of the house for an hour and a half. Susan wanted to take classes at a junior college but Jeff did not allow it. He then became infuriated when Susan went to the campus to enroll anyway, signing up for an Internet course. She had been gone out of the house too long, however, and Jeff became enraged.

"You nasty whore," he screamed as she entered the home. "Are you cheating on me?"

Jeff would smoke marijuana just about every day but according to Susan, the cannabis never took the edge off his personality. She found him to always be easily irritated as anything could set him off. He would complain about problems at work and the utility bills being too high. Then he would single out Susan for keeping a dirty house, fixing a lousy meal or not allowing the kids run around the house screaming.

APPEARANCES CAN BE DECEIVING

On the surface, both Jeff and Susan put on a false front that their home was a place of domestic bliss.

The couple purchased a home in the White Oaks subdivision in the Cypress-Fairbanks area of Houston. This was a fairly affluent area and Jeff was still doing well financially selling carpets and tiles. Another child followed, a daughter they named Kailey, and Susan kept house like a modern day June Cleaver. She entertained friends, family, and neighbors with parties and made sure that her home was the tidiest on the block. Susan had a level of perfectionism which she applied to her home life, she cooked and cleaned, making sure dinner was made and served at the exact same time each day.

Susan also tended the garden and flowers outside the home while Jeff dug out the porch and was in the process of installing a fountain.

Domestic life didn't sit well with Jeff. The cocaine addiction soon got the best of him.

"There were rumors about Jeff," forensic psychologist Paula Orange said. "That he would go to strip clubs and have threesomes with strippers."

Susan knew when Jeff was going on a binge as would become hyperactive, getting too rough with both her and the children. Susan would state that Jeff had kicked, punched and slapped her around during his cocaine-fueled episodes.

"This needs to stop," Susan said as Jeff bounced off the walls in rage.

"You don't fucking tell me what to do," Jeff said, his eyes bleary red. "I'm a grown ass man and you don't give me the rules. I make the fucking rules."

Susan ran to her room.

NO WAY OUT

In the summer of 1999, Jeff had physically beat Susan one night. Susan waited for him to leave the next morning then she packed her bags and took her children to her sister's home. Jeff called her later and told her that a delivery truck was coming by.

"Pack all your stuff back in there," Jeff hissed. "Because if you don't, I will kill you or Bradley."

Fearing for her life, Susan complied.

Jeff's aggression may have been fueled by his cocaine addiction which got the family into financial debt. He also began dating other women.

"He would go through an Internet dating site," Orange said. "He gave Susan herpes. She confronted him about it and he told her that if she 'was a better wife he wouldn't need other women.'"

The belittling and beatings became a daily occurrence as time wore on but Susan never called the police.

"That was a bit problem for the defense during her trial," Orange said. "There were so few people who saw the abuse take place. She had a neighbor who reported that Susan looked terrified of Jeff at times and another who said she saw Jeff grab her by the arm once. But there was never a police report of any kind of domestic disturbance."

Susan would later state that she did not believe in divorce because of her Christian beliefs and that she didn't want to embarrass her family.

But by September of 2002, the marriage was in shambles. Jeff had a new job and wasn't making as much money as before. His cocaine and alcohol addiction had gotten worse. On one occasion, he came home drunk and urinated on their daughter's bed. He then bought an air rifle and hit Susan with the butt of the gun. On New Year's day 2003, his first words to his wife to start off the new year were "Happy fucking New Year, bitch. That will be your last."

THE FINAL STRAW

On the night of January 13th, 2003, Jeff went on another cocaine binge. He then began rough-housing with Bradley, trying to show his young son some boxing moves he learned at the local gym. The horseplay got out of hand as Jeff hit Bradley hard in the face. The boy began to cry and Jeff panicked, fearing Susan would hear.

He waited, fully expecting Susan to come in and investigate.

Minutes passed, then Jeff settled down and laid on the couch, luxuriating in the final hours of his cocaine high.

Susan then came in and took the children to bed. Jeff watched a little television and looked to doze off as the cocaine comedown began.

But his spirits were perked up again when Susan entered the living room wearing nothing more than a silk bathrobe. The light behind her illuminated her curves.

Jeff looked at his young wife with his mouth open. He reached over for the remote and turned off the television, following her into the bedroom without saying a word.

"Susan had enough," Orange said. "She was powerless against the two-hundred twenty pound Jeff in a fight. So she used the one thing that she knew Jeff could not refuse. The one area in their life that she had the power. Sex."

Jeff couldn't help but smile when he entered the bedroom. Susan had gone for an all-out seduction.

Susan looked up at Jeff and smirked as she began lighting red candles around the room. He could not take his eyes off his younger wife as she reached over and pressed play on the CD.

Slow and sexy music filled the air. No words were needed.

Jeff gulped hard. The pleasure of the cocaine buzz and the anticipation of his wife's hot body against his was more than he could bear. Jeff let Susan take the lead in his drug haze and he soon found himself with his back on the bed, buck naked.

Taking a pair of his neck ties, Susan began tying Jeff's arms to the headboard.

"What are you doing, baby?" he asked.

"Shhhh," she whispered as she moved down to his ankles and tied them to the footboard.

Tied down and spread-eagled on the bed, Jeff watched as Susan took one of the candles off the table.

Then she poured the hot wax on his upper thigh.

"The fuck you doing!"

Then she poured the melting wax over his testicles.

"Yaaarrrrgh!" Jeff screamed. "What the fuck!"

He writhed against the knots around his wrists. Susan had done a good job tying him down.

The room was now dimly lit as only a few candle lights remained. Jeff squinted in the darkness as Susan straddled him.

She held up a knife.

"What are you doing!!"

Jeff struggled against the knots again. Susan had done a good job of tying him up. She was a perfectionist.

She did a damn good job.

Jeff felt her take his penis in her hand, pressing the point of the blade against it with the other.

"The hell are you doing?" he screamed, his heart beating out of his chest.

"I've been way too nice to you," Susan said with calm authority. "I played the role of the meek housewife. I let you do what you want. Let you say whatever you want to me. But now, I'm tired. And it's time to turn the tables."

Susan nicked the blade across Jeff's penis.

Screams filled the air.

Susan then placed the point of the blade into his scrotum.

Jeff writhed and pulled against the knots. He could not free himself from the restraints around his wrists and ankles.

Susan then mounted him again and he saw the fiery evil in her eyes.

"Susan," he pleaded. "Please don't."

She stabbed Jeff in the eye first. Then his face and neck.

"She absolutely hated the man," Orange said. "She wanted to completely obliterate his face. It was an act of destruction where she completely wanted to remove his face."

Jeff screamed in pain. Susan began crying and screaming herself, a mixture of a battle cry and years of abuse breaking free. She screamed at Jeff, telling him about every wrong and act of abuse he threw her way.

Susan shrieked as she blitzed Jeff's body with the blade.

Jeff yelped in pain.

All the yelling, however, awoke Bradley.

He knocked on the door.

Susan quickly put on her bathrobe and walked the little boy back to his room.

"Why was daddy screaming?"

"Mommy and daddy are playing a game," Susan said. "Now you get some sleep."

After tucking Bradley back into bed, Susan went back to the bedroom.

Jeff, bloodied from over fifty knife wounds, was still alive.

"None of his wounds," Orange said. "Would have been enough to kill Jeff on its own. So he was laying there in excruciating pain, bleeding out.

Susan then got a second knife from the kitchen, a butcher knife. She returned to the bedroom and resumed her attack, stabbing Jeff another 140 times. The majority were to his face and neck but she attacked his genitals as well.

Tired from the stabbing, Susan caught her breath, waiting for the adrenaline to subside.

"He deserved it," she whispered to herself, trying to rationalize her actions.

Her mind in a fog, she walked over to the bedroom light and flicked it on.

Blood seeped through the bedsheets and was splattered across the walls.

Blood everywhere.

Susan shuddered with panic. There was no way in hell she could clean this mess up.

But she had to survive…And get away with the crime.

She began breaking things down, step by step. The first chore was to go into the shower and get cleaned up. She watched as Jeff's blood dripped off her and into the drain, her thoughts gathering.

Time to cover my ass, she thought, staring at her reflection in the fogged up bathroom mirror.

She then called Jeff's parents who lived over three hours away in Austin. Susan went into melodrama mode as the tears poured out.

"Susan?" Jeff's mother asked. "What is it?"

"It's Jeff," Susan said. "He came home from his boxing lessons and just went wacko."

"What do you mean?"

"He started hitting me," Susan sobbed. "Started hitting Bradley."

"Oh God, no. That's not Jeff."

"He wouldn't stop."

"Put Jeff on the phone."

"He's not here," Susan said. "He just ran out of the house. He's gone for good this time. I know it."

"What was he so angry about?"

"He's on drugs," Susan said. "Has been for a long, long time. Cocaine. Marijuana. Now he has no money and we're in debt because of it. He was just so frustrated all the time but tonight…. Tonight he just went wacko."

"Jeff doesn't do drugs."

"Yes," Susan nodded. "He can't help it. It's a secret."

Susan then remained on the phone with Jeff's parents for over an hour. They tried to console her as she detailed all of his abuses. Finally, she hung up and realized that she had to take care of his body.

But how?

After a few moments, she thought of the fountain out by the back porch. Jeff had left the job unfinished, as per usual, but the hole was pre-dug!

Her adrenaline still pumping, Susan went into the garage and retrieved a dolly that the couple used earlier to roll some new furniture into the house. She untied Jeff's body and plopped him onto the dolly, rolling him down the hall and dropping him face first in the shallow grave next to the back porch.

Another problem arose, however, as Jeff's body had begun to stiffen from the rigor mortis. She bent his legs and torso as much as she could to make him fit in the shallow hole. Then she began pouring the dirt over him.

It would be morning soon and she hurried back into the house. Susan mopped up the blood, starting from the patio, down the hallway and then to the bedroom itself. She rolled up the bloody bed sheets, gagging from the gruesome sight, then placed them into large Hefty bags.

Susan then pulled the mattress from the bed and dragged it into the backyard as she didn't know how to go about cleaning it just yet.

THE NEXT DAY

The children awoke early and Susan took them to daycare. She then drove to the hardware store and purchased a couple gallons of paint.

Arriving back at the house, Susan fought through fatigue and began to clean. She painted the walls and bleached out the blood on the carpet.

After a few hours, everything looked neat and tidy except for a bleach stain on the carpet.

Jeff's parents worried about their son. In the afternoon, they called Susan and asked if Jeff had come back home.

"He came by," Susan said. "Got his stuff and left."

"What do you mean 'got his stuff and left'?"

"He got some clothes," Susan paused, trying to get her story straight. "We started fighting again. He started yelling at me. Got a bottle of bleach and began pouring it around our bedroom. I thought he was going to set the place on fire."

"He wouldn't do that."

"He did," Susan said, adamant.

"We need to talk to him."

"He left his cell phone here," Susan said.

After the next few hours, Susan would field calls from Jeff's employer and a neighbor. She told Jeff's boss that he had gone "wacko" and told the neighbor the same story she had told Jeff's parents.

The neighbor advised Susan to call the police.

Susan realized that the noose around her neck would close fast if she didn't do something. She had to take the initiative somehow to get ahead of the investigation as Jeff's parents and the police would have plenty of questions.

First, she went to the emergency room and reported that she had been beaten by Jeff.

The doctor on duty at the time, Stephen Fischer, stated that he believed Susan and told her to report the injuries to the police. Later, under cross-examination, the prosecutor got Dr. Fischer to admit that he really didn't know how Susan got those injuries and was going strictly off what he told her.

On January 15th, 2003, two days after she had murdered Jeff, Susan entered Precinct Four of the Harris County Constable's office. She filed a report on Jeff, once again using the same story that she had told his parents and her neighbor.

She had physical evidence to back up her story as she had cuts on her hands and a bruise on her thigh.

"I'm scared of what will happen when he comes back," Susan informed the reporting officer. "He's abusive and violent."

A restraining order against Jeff was filed.

"She had a bruise on her thigh," Orange said. "The police chalked up her complaint as a routine domestic violence case."

A WEB OF DECEIT

Three days later, however, Susan felt the pressure of her lies. Jeff's parents kept calling, family and friends, plus his employer.

There was no way she could keep up this charade.

Looking out the window, she saw their dog, a chow mix, had dug up the area where Jeff had been buried. She could see the dog had unearthed Jeff's arm as well as the back of his head.

The chow had tried to pull its owner from its burial place, however, and in doing so had bitten off Jeff's hand.

The dog played with the hand as if it were a toy, laying it on the patio.

It was a sick irony, as Jeff would often beat the dog and once threw it against the wall.

But the visual of her husband's half-buried body and dismembered hand sent Susan into a panic.

She needed to tell someone.

Susan placed her daughter Kailey and son Bradley into her car and headed straight toward her mother's house.

She told her mother the same story as before, informing her about the restraining order.

"He'll kill me if he comes back," Susan said. Her voice was now half-hearted. She had to tell someone. If she was going to come clean, it would have to be with her mother first.

"Susan, you really need to tell me what's going on."

"It wasn't just a fight," Susan said to her mother, fighting back tears. "And he didn't just run away."

"What do you mean?"

"He's dead."

"You're overreacting."

"No," Susan said. " I stabbed him. I buried him in the backyard. I didn't know what else to do."

Susan slumped forward and put her head on the table, sobbing.

Her mother called Susan's sister Cindy to come pick up the children. She then had to save her daughter at all costs, calling up numerous defense attorneys to price them accordingly.

Her mother hired Neal Davis, who came to the home. He then informed the police of Jeff's body in the back yard.

The police searched the home and found evidence of blood that Susan had failed to clean during her bleach wash.

THE TRIAL

The case took over thirteen months to reach a trial which started on February 24th, 2004.

Susan would stake the stand and claim self-defense.

"Susan had a rough go of it in the trial," Orange said. "Every part of it was televised and she was going up against a prosecuting attorney named Kelly Siegler. Siegler was ferocious and often used out of the box methods to defeat defense attorneys."

Once the trial began, Siegler immediately pounced on Susan like Mike Tyson trying to finish his foe in the first few seconds of a fight.

The first question Siegler asked Susan was "Have you ever lied to avoid getting into trouble?"

"No," Susan said in an unsure voice "I can't say I ever have."

"Siegler's tactic was to show Susan to be the liar she was," Orange said. "Everyone on the jury has lied before. Show right off the bat, the prosecution hit a home run."

"He attacked me with a knife," Susan said. "He kept yelling 'Die, bitch! Die bitch!'"

"Why did you stab him almost 200 times?" the prosecutor asked.

"Once I started," Susan began to cry. "I couldn't stop. If I stopped, he would have killed me."

Siegler then called Susan's tears "fake." She argued that Susan killed Jeff in order to collect on a $200,000 life insurance policy.

Siegler then had the Wright's actual bed brought into the courtroom. The prosecutor asked a younger male member of her staff to lay on the bed while she re-enacted the murder for the jury. The man struggled against the restraints much like Jeff would have. Siegler then proceeded to "stab the victim" over and over again...197 times...stimulating Susan's act down to the very last stroke of the blade.

The jury was shaken by this visual. They would deliberate over five and a half-hours before declaring that Susan was guilty of murder.

"She stabbed Jeff at least 197 times," Orange said. "I say at least 197 times because the coroners determined that she stabbed him in numerous spots more than once. They couldn't determine the exact amount."

Susan's married life had echoed what she saw in her own childhood when she witnessed her mother go through nightly beat downs at the hands of her father. Susan's mother would later deny this but Susan's sister, Cindy, would confirm that their mother was indeed the victim of abuse. Cindy had a Ph.D., in psychology and would state that witnessing these beatings left a scar in Susan's memories that she could never erase.

"She stabbed Jeff for all the times that he punched her in the chest, and she stabbed him for all of the times that he raped her in the middle of the night. And she stabbed Jeff because he was just like her father."

In March of 2004, Susan would be sentenced to 25 years to left for killing Jeff Wright.

Things took a turn in her favor, however, when Misty McMichael came forward and relayed her experience with Jeff Wright. McMichael was another former stripper who had dated Jeff for four years and verified that she had been the victim of his violence and abuse.

The Fourteenth Court of Appeals of Texas then gave Susan a new hearing.

A video recording of Bradley was brought in as evidence for the new trial. Bradley was filmed in 2003 by Harris County Child Protective Services when he was four-years-old. In the video, Bradley was working on a coloring book.

"Have you ever seen your dad hit your mom?" the interviewer asked.

"No," Bradley said.

"Did you ever see bruises on your mom?"

"She has some on her legs."

"How did she get them?"

"I don't know."

The prosecution would later try to insinuate that Susan had drugged Jeff, noting the level of GHB (the 'date rape' drug) in her system. The toxicology report would reveal had Jeff had used cocaine but less than .1 gram was in his body. There was also 33 mg of GHB found but this is a naturally occurring chemical which exacerbates as the body decomposes. The toxicologist could only say there was a "fifty-fifty" chance that GHB was administered to Jeff during the night of his murder.

Kevin Conboy, one of Jeff's co-workers, would be called to testify at the re-sentencing trial. The prosecution wanted to reiterate the fact that Susan was overly concerned about Jeff's life insurance policy.

"It was clear that the conversation was about the insurance policy and whether or not Jeff had turned in the insurance policy," Conboy said. "That he would get it taken care of and he would turn in paperwork and he also said, 'If I die, you will be a very rich woman."

This go around, however, the defense team would make sure the jury knew about Susan's abuse. They would call on one of Jeff's brother-in-laws, Brian Roberts, who witnessed a fight between the couple.

"I saw her turn to Jeff with a knife," Roberts said.

He also claimed that he spoke to Susan about Jeff's abuse.

"I asked her if it had happened before."

"What was her answer?" the defense attorney asked.

"'Yes, 2,3,5 more than 6 times,' she said."

Kay Wright, Jeff's mother, would take the stand as well.

"He said, 'I love you, Mom'" Kay said, fighting back tears as she described her son's last words to her. She informed the jury that she had no reason to believe that Susan was lying when she said she kicked out Jeff during that fateful evening.

"I said, 'Has Jeff come back?' And she said, 'Yes he's come back.' And she said he got some of his clothes and he took my clothes and put bleach all over them in the bedroom and she also said he'd left a note that said thanks for betraying me or something like that. She said, 'If anything ever happens to me, I want my kids to live with my sister.' I said, 'Nothing is going to happen. Jeffrey will come home and we'll straighten this thing out."

Kay listened to all of this not knowing that her son Jeff lay dead, stabbed nearly 200 times just a few feet away from Susan.

But the defense had a better case this go around. The twenty-five-year punishment was reversed. Susan had been given leeway as she convinced the jury that she suffered from battered women syndrome.

"At the end of the day," Orange said. "This was an impulse murder. Susan had to tie Jeff down and most likely drug him up. Helpless and not knowing what else to do, she committed one of the most brutal murders I had ever studied. But she was not a psychopath. She was an abused woman who snapped and did something psychopathic. That doesn't mean that she shouldn't be duly punished. And it doesn't necessarily mean that she's a psychopath frothing at the mouth."

They would take off five years from Susan's sentence and make her eligible for parole.

"If we are to believe that Susan's allegations of abuse are true," Orange said. "Then she definitely was a poster child for battered women's syndrome. In other words, she could not leave Jeff whenever anyone looking at the situation objectively would. She acquired a learned state of helplessness. She lost hope at her ability to change the situation. There are some psychologists who believe that the battered woman can become homicidal when they are pushed to the brink. When Susan saw her son being hit by Jeff, she lost it."

Bradley and Kailey would later be adopted by Jeff's brother, Ronald.

# BLONDE BUTCHER : The True Story of Ruth Judd

ERIN SPENCER

In 1931, Winnie Ruth Judd killed two of her best friends then cut one of them into pieces. She packed their remains inside two storage trunks and boarded a train for Los Angeles with the dead bodies as "luggage".

The media circus surrounding her crime was a parallel of the O.J. Simpson case in the mid-1990s. Reporters and readers alike were hungry for every sordid detail. Ruth, as she was known to her friends, would be tried and sentenced for execution until being declared mentally incompetent. She would later be remanded to the care of the Arizona State mental hospital where she would "escape" over seven times. During her last escape, she would journey to northern California where she would adopt an alias and avoid detection for over six years before her recapture.

# CHAPTER ONE – EARLY LIFE

Winnie Judd was born Winnie Ruth McKinnell on January 29th, 1905. Born in Oxford, Indiana, her family soon moved from town to town as her father preached in different Methodist churches.

She suffered from tuberculosis as a child and was sent to an Arizona sanitarium for care. It was there that the seventeen year old would meet a thirty-seven year old physician named William Judd. They two would marry and Ruth would accompany him to Mexico where he was employed as a medic for American silver miners.

William, a World War I veteran, became a morphine addict in trying to cope with his injuries. The addiction soon seeped into his business life and he began having trouble holding down a job. The couple returned to the United States and began moving from city to city. The marriage was not a happy one as Ruth could not produce children and had repeated bouts with tuberculosis while William continued to struggle with his morphine addiction.

By 1930, the couple had a "needle separation", living apart but still remaining on talking terms. Winnie who had usually been called by her middle name, Ruth, had moved to Phoenix, Arizona where she hoped the drier climate would help with her tuberculosis. She had found work as a nanny to children with the Leigh Ford family, who were well-to-do. Upon her arrival in Phoenix, she met John "Happy Jack" Halloran, a successful businessman.

Halloran was married but was known for having open affairs.

John Halloran was nicknamed "Happy Jack" by the press when they got wind of his philandering ways. He was the co-founder of Halloran Bennett Lumber Company. A jowly man with a jovial personality, he used his wealth and status to procure young "party girls" despite the fact that he was married.

The two met while Ruth worked as a nanny for the Leigh Ford family. Jack lived next door with his wife and spotted the frail but pretty Ruth sitting on the Ford's front porch. He engaged the young woman in conversation and found out that her husband was away at a rehab center fighting another bout against his morphine addiction. Ruth confided to Jack that she was lonely and the opportunistic philanderer made his move.

Their affair began on Christmas Eve of 1930 up until the night she murdered Anne and Sammy who were also involved with Jack.

Winnie would quit her job with the Ford family and obtain work as a medical secretary at the Grunow Medical Clinic in Phoenix.

It is here where she would befriend Agnes "Anne" Leroi, an x-ray technician and her roommate Hedvig "Sammy" Samuelson.

The two women had moved to Phoenix from Alaska as they wanted a better climate after Sammy had contracted tuberculosis.

The trio would have a tumultuous friendship that hinted of a love triangle between Annie, Ruth and Jack as well as a hints of homosexuality.

# CHAPTER TWO – A TRIANGLE OF LUST

Ruth become close with Annie and Sammy, often having sleepovers at their bungalow. The two women soon become friends with Jack who, being the philanderer that he was, quickly indulged in relations with Annie.

This didn't sit well with Ruth who mistakenly believed that Jack loved her.

On October 16th, 1931, neighbors heard screaming coming from the bungalow. But the yelling stopped as quickly as it started and no one reported the fracas.

"I had introduced Jack to a girl they (Annie/Sammy) objected to," Winnie said in a jailhouse interview. "That is what the quarrel was over. He (Halloran) was a friend of my husband but he was trying to kiss my behind my husband's back. And I loved my husband very much."

Ruth had shot both women in a jealous fit with a .25 caliber handgun.

She then dismembered Sammy's body and put her head, torso, and lower legs into a shipping trunk while placing her thighs in a traveling suitcase. Annie's body was not dismembered, instead being stuffed into another shipping trunk.

The morning after, Ruth showed up late for work at the clinic while her co-workers wondered about the whereabouts of Annie. Later at the trial, some workers reported seeing Ruth as having a bandage on her left hand. Some remembered it being on her right. Others didn't remember it at all.

After her shift ended, Ruth called a moving van to retrieve a pair of large trunks and have them placed on a train for Los Angeles two days after the murders.

Ruth boarded the Golden State Limited passenger train at Phoenix's Union Station with both the trunk and suitcase which contained the bodies. She arrived in Los Angeles but her trunks immediately brought suspicion as porters saw the "stained fluid" coming from the trunks which was emitting a foul smell as well.

The porter, a man named Arthur Anderson, confronted Ruth.

"Ma'am," the porter said. "There's something leaking out of your trunk."

"Is there?"

"You know, a lot of folks try to transport contraband into Los Angeles," the train agent continued. "I've seen it all. Had one big game hunter use his wife to transport a dead deer. You wouldn't do something like that would you?"

"God, no."

"Do you have the keys for the trunk?"

"Its in my car."

"Let's open it please."

"My car is just outside," Ruth said, heading out of the depot. "Just wait right here. I'll get my keys, unlock the trunk and then I'll see what's leaking."

Ruth's younger brother Burton arrived in his vehicle to pick her up. Burton, a USC college student, had no idea that Ruth just committed murder.

"Drive," Ruth commanded.

"Where's all your stuff?" Burton asked.

"Just drive, Burton! Don't ask any questions, just go."

The car sped away as Anderson stepped out of the depot. He had the presence of mind to memorize the license plate of the vehicle and immediately reported the incident to the Los Angeles Police Department.

The police arrived, picked the locks on each of the trunks and were shocked to discovered the dead bodies inside.

"I was the chief investigator of the case," retired Phoenix detective Charles Arnold said. "From the police department in Phoenix at the time it happened. At the time it happened, the Phoenix police department knew nothing of Ruth Judd. Never heard of her. Until our police chief, that morning, received a call about nine o'clock, received a call from the captain of homicide from Los Angeles. The chief had said that they had discovered these trunks with nude bodies in them at the depot."

The police traced the car to Ruth's brother but the woman herself had disappeared. Ruth had gone home with Burton then hid in a department store among other places.

# CHAPTER THREE – THE TRUNK MURDERS

The horrific crime would send shock waves throughout the country. The press would refer to Winnie as "Tiger Woman", "Blonde Butcher", and finally the case became known simply as the "Trunk Murders."

On Monday, October 19th, 1931, the Phoenix police force entered the home of Agnes and Sammy. Neighbors and reporters were also on the premises, disturbing the crime scene. The next day, the landlord of the bungalow placed an advertisement in two newspapers informing the public that he would be doing tours of the crime scene for ten cents per person.

Because of the ad, hundreds of people came through the bungalow out of morbid curiosity.

With their forensic evidence now contaminated, police nonetheless believed that both Annie and Sammy were shot while asleep in their beds. Both of their mattresses were missing from the bungalow but one was later found in a vacant lot a few miles away with no blood on it. The other mattress remained missing.

Police would also find a letter that Ruth had written to her husband but never mailed. The letter described a multitude of sexual goings-on at the Phoenix bungalow. Ruth would detail straight, bisexual and homosexual trysts that the trio would engage in.

With his wife now a wanted woman, Dr. William Judd put forth a public appeal for his Ruth to turn herself in.

Winnie caught word of her wanted status and would meet with police on October 23rd in a Los Angeles funeral home.

Detective Arnold led the interrogation of Ruthie as they spoke to her in the funeral home.

"Mrs, Judd, don't you think if a doctor amputated these bodies he would have known where to cut them and had to cut four and five places to find the joint?" Arnold asked.

Ruth shifted in her seat. "Well, it wasn't the doctor. I'll tell you who it was. It was Jack Halloran. Jack helped."

"How did you get the mattress out to the vacant lot that the women were laying on when you shot them?"

"I never shot no woman on a mattress!"

"Oh, yea, Ruthie, you shot women on the mattress. Because we found a mattress out on a vacant lot where you set it afire. And it hadn't burned up. And that was where the two women were laying side by each on this mattress. Because the blood spots were in two different spots on the mattress. And now, matter of fact, these women were sound asleep when you shot them weren't they?"

"No, no, they were fighting me."

"Ruthie, they wasn't fighting you. How could they be fighting you when you had them both in the bed there and you shot them straight down through the bed because the gunshots went through the mattress? How do you account for that Ruthie?"

Ruthie sat and stared at the ground. "Well, Jack Halloran helped me do it. And he said I should do that in order to get rid of the bodies."

"I said a while ago you told us that a doctor did that. Now Ruthie your story is all wet," Arnold shifted forward in his seat, narrowing his eyes. "Let me tell you the story. You went out there with this gun to kill these women because this one woman had rejected your love isn't that right? You found them sound asleep and you had the key to the door so you went quietly in there to where they were sleeping and you shot them right through the bed there. Because on this mattress that you drug out to the vacant lot and tried to burn there's two spots of blood not one, not a big spot, not a little spot but two spots in the mattress where the hole went through. Ain't that right, Ruthie?"

Tears began to well in Ruth's eyes. She gulped hard.

"Then you cut them up back there in the bath tub, you want to make this story good about fighting so I said you shot yourself through the hand, didn't you?"

"No, no, no, I never had any gun."

"Oh yes, Ruthie, you had a gun. A little automatic. Same gun you shot the women with. I found the bullet under bathtub that you shot yourself through the hand with."

Ruth broke down and began to cry. "I'm not telling you anything. I'm not saying anything. I'm not talking to you again, ever!"

Upon her arrest, Ruth became the O.J. Simpson of her day. The people of the 1930s were unused to the immorality depicted in Judd's crime-murder, infidelity, lesbianism, and drug use. They was conjecture that Agnes "Anne" and Hedvig "Sammy" Samuelson were "lesbian party girls" who seduced Ruth into their lifestyle of debauchery and perversion along with their mutual boyfriend, Jack Halloran.

# CHAPTER FOUR – SELF DEFENSE OR PRE-MEDIATION?

Ruth would describe her murders of Annie and Sammy as incidents of self-defense. She described getting into an altercation with Sammy initially, describing how Sammy took out a gun and threatened to blow her brains out. Ruth said that she fought back and they both struggled with the gun.

"I went into the kitchen to set down some tapioca dessert," Winnie recalled. "We were all in our pajamas. I went to put this down on the sink and Sammy came at me with a gun. She came through the breakfast room door."

"We quarreled violently," Winnie said. "About what I was going to tell about them and what they were going to tell my husband about me and so forth. That I had gone out with Jack. So the fact that it took place in the breakfast room door. I'm naturally left handed. I do many things with my left hand. I grabbed the gun with this hand (her left) and the shot went through there (her palm.)And I grabbed a bread knife on the table and I stabbed her twice in the (left) shoulder. And the knife bent, it was a bread knife, so I grabbed her hand like this (pulling her wrist back) and we both had our hands on the gun and one shot went through one of her fingers. I don't know which one. And one went through her chest. And one bullet jammed and caught me here (her left ring finger), at the top of the gun. And Ann came from behind. She got the ironing board from behind the water heater and came up behind me and hit me which caused us both to fall in the doorway. And we fought back and forth, wrestling for the gun in the door way, both of us on the floor. And the blood was all underneath the linoleum that was the only way it got there it was from the fight. She was not shot in bed like they say! It was in the doorway and the kitchen. It wasn't in the bedroom at all."

Ruth then called Jack to help dispose of the dead bodies.

"Jack cut up Sammy's body," Ruth said initially. "I couldn't do it."

She would later recant on that claim and state that Jack Halloran had called up a "Dr. Brown" and had him come over to cut up the bodies. She said that Halloran had some "dirt" on the doctor which coerced the physician to come over to the home and become complicit in the murder.

"Jack came with me," Ruth said. "And he picked Sammy up and carried her in (to the bed). And he got Doctor Brown. They took me home because I was hysterical."

Ruth would also claim later that she had gone to Anne and Sammy's home for a game of bridge. A fourth woman was there but had left. She testified that there was an argument about Halloran's introduction to another woman and that Annie and Sammy attacked her.

Ruth stated that Halloran came to the bungalow and after seeing the bodies, began plotting a way to "fix things". He went to the garage and came back with a "great, heavy trunk".

"Don't say a word to anyone," he warned her.

Halloran would be blamed for being an accomplice in the crime but after further research the decision not to prosecute him seemed to be the right one, particularly with the half-baked imagination of Ruth.

Her stories would remain inconsistent during her interrogation with Detective Arnold as well.

"So we interviewed her for about an hour," Arnold recalled. "And she'd tell us one story and we'd head her off on that. And then she'd sit there for a few minutes and she'd say well, 'That's right, but I'm gonna tell you the truth now!' And she'd tell us another story. We asked her 'where's the knife that you used to cut these women up with?' 'I never cut no women up!' 'Oh yes, yes you must have because there were in your trunk. Where's the knife?' 'I never had any knife.' 'Well who cut the women up?' 'Well, the doctor cut 'em up.' 'A doctor helped you cut them up?' 'No, a doctor cut them up. He was there. He's my friend.'

It was discovered during the investigation that Jack Halloran and Ruth were having an affair. Halloran himself became under suspicion for the killings and was indicted by a grand jury on December 30th, 1932.

Ruth would become the primary witness through a preliminary hearing which lasted three days.

*"I am going to be hanged for something Jack Halloran is responsible for,"* Winnie said. *"I was convicted of murder, but I shot in self-defense[1]. Jack Halloran removed every bit of evidence. He is responsible for me going through all this. He is guilty of anything I am guilty of."*

Even Dr. Judd, the husband of Ruth, believed that the man with whom is wife cheated with was not capable of the crime.

"I know Jack Halloran," Dr. Judd said. "And it is very difficult for me to believe that Jack had anything to do with that."

Halloran did not bother to take the stand during his hearing. His attorney informed the court that Ruth's stories were the rantings of a crazy woman. He argued further that since Winnie claimed that she killed the two women in self-defense there was no crime committed and Halloran was guilty of nothing.

The judge agreed, freeing Halloran in the belief that putting him to trial would be "an idle gesture."

"Jack Halloran had no more to do with the case than I did," Detective Arnold said. "She tried to involve Jack Halloran to get him to finance her defense. And when she fell down on it well, naturally she told a story that Jack helped her cut up the bodies and so on. But she already told that a doctor that helped her but she never would give us the doctor's name."

The controversy surrounding the case did irreparable damage to Halloran's reputation. He would lose valuable business contacts and

---

1.      *https://en.wikipedia.org/wiki/Self-defense*

his social standing in the community. Six years later, he would die at
suddenly at the age of fifty-two.

# CHAPTER FIVE – A LETTER OF CONFESSION

In 1931, Ruth would write out her "true confession" letter below and deliver it to her attorney. This letter detailed both the events of the night of the murder and her thought processes. Her attorney, Howard Richardson, did not use the letter. He instead had it "buried" as he tried to get her off on an insanity plea.

*"I am writing the absolute truth of this case, in full confidence, that you will use it as you see fit in your best judgment. Mr. Richardson, I have full confidence in you and trust you.*

*This is my first and only confession of the case of the homicide of Anne LeRoi and Hedvig Samuelson. Anne was used to the world, I truly was not. Jack was the only man I had gone with since my marriage. I was ashamed of things I had done. I could not openly compete with her, I was married and ashamed to. Day after day she lorded it over me, always smiling and fresh and sweet, well knowing she was hurting me with her taunts. Many evenings Anne would kiss Jack and caress him in our presence, then after he was gone gloat over not caring a thing for him but merely working him for money. It was not what Jack did but the continual taunts made by Anne which drove me beside myself. . . . I could not stand taunts. I just went crazy. Those taunts kept me awake, I could not sleep. I cried. I even prayed. I wrote my parents to please come to me. I was losing my mind. Wild ideas kept me awake. I took sleeping sedatives, Luminal. I wrote Doctor my nerves were breaking. I couldn't eat. I couldn't sleep. I loved Anne still, but those taunts. I would take more medicine to quiet my nerves, cried to please get things off my mind, to sleep. Friday night I expected Jack. He did not come. I went to bed. Again I could not sleep. I got up, went over to Anne's house. My brain whirling. I was so excited I was panting for breath. Never did I have the slightest dream of hurting Sammy. She simply never entered my mind. Except to get Anne, stop those taunts so I could sleep. Nothing more did I think of. I took the gun and a knife. How I would do it I was not sure. But I had no intention of harming Sammy. Jack was as intimate with Sammy as Anne, but it was Anne's cruel taunts that haunted me. . . . I hid in the house next door. Anne and Sammy returned to the bedroom . . . After they retired, I went to the back door, laid the knife and my shoes outside the door, then crept in the unlocked front door . . . I sat down on the couch in the same dark room and soon fell to sleep clutching the gun. I awakened, Sammy had gone to the bathroom, that insane desire, that power lead me on, I started for Anne. My stomach was turning inside out really twitching, jumping out of me, outside not a tremor, but my stomach jumping like convulsions. I retreated, curled up and went to sleep again. I went back to sleep again. Oh again and again all night I don't know how many times. Sammy kept going to the bathroom, I started for that bedroom and retreated each time so exhausted I immediately went to sleep.*

*Morning! I heard the milk man. Sammy went to the bathroom again. I started to call her, tell her I was there. I really did. Then I began shaking inside and remembered what I had come to do so this time I crept past the bathroom door, shot Anne. It was a low shot. Sammy called, What fell, Anne? I was hurrying past the door Sammy came out demanded to know what was the matter. I was limp she completely took the gun from my hands. I was non-resistant. I said, Sammy, I am crazy. I have lost my mind give me that gun and I will blow my brains out right here in this door. She held the gun and said, you get out of here right this minute.*

*... I then picked up the knife and went back after her with the knife. As I grabbed for the gun, I stabbed her in the shoulder, the fight with Sammy in that breakfast room door; her own finger on the trigger when the shot went through her chest; our fight is all about as I have always related she shot me through the hand as I grabbed for the gun; the gun jammed; we fell to the floor, struggled and I finally got the gun and shot her and in my wild state I really do not remember where in the head. I pulled Sammy into the bathroom. I cleaned up the floor I pulled in the*

*trunk from the garage. It was now about 6:30 or 7 a.m. . . . I tugged and pulled and finally got Anne from the bed into the trunk. Now it doesn't sound possible but this all took about two hours. I left for the office . . . I had pulled the trunk with Anne's body into the living room. But the trunk was unlocked. Sammy was on the bathroom floor all day Saturday . . . This all happened in the morning. I stayed in my office . . . until 4 p.m. I then took the bag home with me with the gun, knife, pajamas and dress. I fed my cat and went back to the 2929 N. 2nd Street house at around 6 p.m. I really had nothing definite in my mind. No plans made. In fact except for an irresistible impulse to get Anne I had no other plans. I entered the house through the bathroom window getting a chair from next door to climb in. I pulled the trunk back into the hall tried to lift Sammy into it, but that was utterly impossible, I couldn't possibly lift her, she was too heavy her body was stiff. I then got two cheap knives from the kitchen and severed her body into portions I could lift. I was hours doing this and then inch by inch pulling the trunk back into the living room."*

# CHAPTER SIX – THE TRIAL

Three months after the bodies had been discovered, Judd's trial began. Ruth would not be tried for the murder of Sammy, only the murder of Agnes.

Richardson would be steadfast in his defense that Ruth was innocent by reason of insanity. He didn't allow her to take the stand. He kept the existence of Ruth's confessional letter to himself.

The case went to trial with the prosecutors taking aim at Ruth's self-defense alibi. They pointed out the fact that Ruth did not have a bullet wound in her hand when she showed up for work the day after and that her wound was, in fact, self-inflicted to confuse authorities. They further argued that Ruth killed the two women out of a jealous rage as she did not want her husband to find out about her affair with Jack Halloran.

The jurors agreed with the prosecution and found Ruth guilty of two counts of first-degree murder.

She was sentenced to death by hanging.

Ruth then behaved oddly in jail, screaming, yelling and making bizarre gestures. Because of her high-profile case, the Arizona governor gave her a special sanity hearing that took place only three days before her scheduled death-by-hanging.

This hearing became a spectacle for the media. Ruth put on a show, laughing inappropriately, clapping her hands, screaming obscenities at the jury and pulling out clumps of her hair. She then tried to take off her clothes and had to be restrained.

"She's been crazy all her life," Ruth's mother would testify during the hearing. "More or less."

"She comes from a long, lineage of crazy folk," Winnie's father, the Methodist preacher revealed. "Our family has been cursed with madness for over 125 years. It goes all the way back to Scotland."

The testimony worked and Ruth's death sentence was commuted to a life prison term. She was then sent to an Arizona state hospital for the criminally insane.

# CHAPTER SEVEN – FUGITIVE ON THE RUN

Ruth would show a dramatic improvement in her mental stability during her stay at the hospital. She no longer displayed the same screaming fits or displays of anger. She fit in with the prison population and embrace the routine, all the while calculating ways to escape.

She left behind a "dummy" in her bed, made up of items around the sanitarium. Fooling the guards, she slipped out of the mental hospital only to be recaptured days later.

The prison guards had her on close watch upon her return but Ruth was determined.

She would escape a total of seven times. On one occasion, Ruth walked all the way from Phoenix to Yuma, Arizona, making her way along the Southern Pacific railroad tracks. These escapes would become a national joke because on slow news days reporters would remark, "maybe Winnie Ruth Judd will escape again."

These escapes would become a running gag among the more sensationalist newspapers. One magazine opened an article on Judd with the words : "When you read this story, the country's cleverest maniac may be at large again, perhaps walking down your street, or sitting next to you."

Ruth would return to her sanitarium after another escape in 1952. Inexplicably, she would be called to testify before a grand jury that was investigating state hospital conditions.

Ever the opportunist, Ruth would plot out another escape during her transport to the hearing. She was searched beforehand, however, and prison guards found a key hidden in her hair and a razor blade concealed beneath her tongue.

A year later, Ruth would have another sanity hearing. During this time she would spent a great deal of time trying to obtain her letter of confession back from her attorney Howard Robinson's widow to get this letter back. She had enough wherewithal to realize that if the letter would be made public it would be incriminating evidence against her insanity defense.

Richardson's widow did not comply but the letter would not be revealed until after Ruth's death.

# CHAPTER EIGHT – THE GREAT ESCAPE

Ruth would stage her most successful escape on October 8th, 1963.

She coerced a friend to give her the key to the front door of the hospital and made her way out undetected in the middle of the night.

"About these seven escapes," Arnold said. "The woman, in my opinion, its just my opinion, but I've been around. This woman never escaped out there. She was turned loose every time she went away from that asylum. They wanted to get rid of her! And she wasn't getting seen very fast according to their opinion. And every time she went out of there she'd go out and try to get money from some of her old friends to leave town on and she couldn't get the money. Then somebody would see her and turn her in and then of course the hospital would have to go back and get her. And put her back in the hospital. And that was carried on there for a number of years as I say as everybody knows she's supposedly escaped from there seven times. Before she got enough money to leave town on (laughs)."

Ruth somehow made her way from the Arizona sanitariums to the San Francisco Bay Area where she took on the name of "Marian Lane."

She lived with the wealthy Nichols family, finding work as their live-in maid.

"One of the reasons I came here (to San Francisco) was to be near him (her husband)," Winnie said. "He's buried here in the Golden Gate National Military Cemetery. And when I go down there frequently, I put violets on his grave. I thought he was a wonderful person. He was ill and he was worth saving. And I worked very hard. Ms. Nickles knew I loved violets so she had a whole lot planted so I could pick them anytime and take them to his grave. Because I was buying violets and she said I'll plant the violets, she was that kind and good to me."

Her identity was eventually discovered and she was recaptured after six years of freedom. Ruth would hire attorney Melvin Belli to represent her and he fought her extradition to Arizona. Governor Ronald Reagan, however, personally intervened, sending Ruth back to Arizona.

Ruth would be tried again and judged sane, thus ending her stays at sanitariums. She was sent to jail but only incarcerated for an additional two years.

Ruth would be paroled on December 22$^{nd}$, 1971. Upon her release she moved to Stockton, California where she lived out the rest of her life without incident. In 1983, the state of Arizona gave her an "absolute discharge" which meant that she was no longer a parolee of the state.

Winnie Ruth Judd would die on October 23$^{rd}$, 1998 at the age of ninety-three.

# AMELIA DYER

JANET COLE

Amelia Dyer, considered one of the most prolific serial killers in history, was born around 1837 in Victorian Britain. Her picture on the front cover easily betrays the evil that resided within her heart. Her reign of terror lasted over twenty years, as she is projected to have killed as many as 400 children before finally being caught

She embarked on a thirty year career of killing with eyewitnesses seeing at least six babies entering her house a day. The count of 400 dead is a conservative estimate.

EARLY LIFE

Amelia was the youngest of five children born into the tiny town of Pyle Marsh. She had three older brothers, Thomas, James, and William along with an older sister named Ann. Her father was a shoemaker named Samuel Hobley and her mother was named Sarah Weymouth.

But he didn't come from an impoverished family like so many others during the Victorian Era.

"For the time, she had a pretty good start," said author Allison Rattle. "Her father had a pretty good trade and paid for her to go to church and school which at the time only a quarter of the children her age actually got an education so she was privileged in that respect."

She found entertainment in reading and used to write poetry herself. Amelia's mother Sarah, however, became mentally ill after suffering from typhus fever. Amelia had to suffer through watching her mother's seizures and outbursts, providing care for her until she died in 1848.

"She witnessed her mother basically losing her mind," said Rattle. "And dying a slow, horrific death. I guess being a young girl she may have been called upon to nurse her mother slightly or at least wait upon her."

Psychologists have posited that it was going through this trauma of watching her mother lose her mind, that caused Amelia's own emotional wiring to run askew.

"Amelia would later claim that her mother died as a result of hereditary insanity," said author Allison Vale. "I think though that this isn't true but it's really easy to understand how she could have remembered it that way."

"It was certain to have a massive impact on her and she may have learned a few things about what kind of symptoms might be shown by someone whose losing their mind."

Amelia was sent to live with her aunt in nearby Bristol after her mother's death. She started an apprenticeship with a corset maker and worked there until her father died in 1859. The oldest brother, Thomas, took control of the family shoe business. Two years later, some type of estrangement occurred with her brothers, specifically James and Amelia doesn't appear to have further ties with her family.

In 1861, Amelia moved to Trinity Street, Bristol. She married George Thomas, who at 59 years old was 35 years Amelia's senior. The two lied about their ages on their marriage certificate with George claiming he was 48 years old and Amelia claiming she was 30.

A CAREER IN "HEALTH CARE"

Amelia began training as a nurse after she got married.

"Amelia turned to one of the most arduous professions she could have turned to," Vale said. "Nursing was just starting to change. It was post-Crimean war. Nursing was starting to have a much better profile as a result of Florence Nightingale. But it was still a thankless profession."

"It wasn't a caring profession like it is present day," agreed psychologist Laura Richards. "They train you psychologically to be a lot more robust around dealing with people. So she became quite hardy and emotionless from having been trained through the nursing regime."

Amelia became pregnant at the age of twenty-six before she met a woman named Ellen Dane who came to boarder at her house. Dane was a midwife who told her of a lucrative and shady way to earn money. Amelia would use her own home as a front to provide housing for women who had gotten pregnant out of wedlock. They would them give the babies away for adoption or kill them through malnutrition.

They called it baby farming.

"Amelia could see it was a very easy way to make money," Rattle said. "Although with risks involved obviously although Amelia did have training as a mid-wife as well through her nursing experience so it was certainly something she knew she was capable of doing. That was the beginning of a massive change in Amelia's life."

Dane moved her base of operations to the USA while Amelia took her "business plan" to heart. During this time, unmarried mothers did not have access to any kind of subsidy as the 1834 Poor Law Amendment Act did not oblige the fathers of illegitimate children to pay for their upbringing. These laws, coupled with the stigmatization of single mothers, forced the practice of baby farming.

Amelia discussed business strategies with Dane. She knew the best bet was to insist on being paid upfront with a one-time fee. She refused any type of money for continuous care as she knew that would mean the mother would return to visit.

"The one off premiums were certainly not enough to sustain a child's life for long financially," Vale said. "And the only way that it would be profitable for a baby farmer was to subject a child to persist underfeeding that would at some point bring about the infant's death."

"Abortion was not an option," Judith Knelman said. "So the simplest thing to do was hide, have the baby and get rid of it. Pay somebody to take care of it or pay somebody to get rid of it."

The babies were subsequently left on the premises and seen as "nurse children."

"Illegitimacy was seen as hugely immoral," said author Allison Rattle. "Even orphanages would only accept orphans from families where the parents were married and the father had died. They wouldn't accept a child who was born out of wedlock."

"Dickens did a really good job of describing social conditions in the 1850 and 60s," Knelman added. "Certainly there were a lot of poor people. There were a lot of neglected and abandoned children."

"There was no work," said Alan McCormick of Scotland Yard. "There was no social services. There was no welfare. One in every twelve women was a prostitute. A child being born in normal circumstances only had a fifty percent chance of reaching the age of five. So that's how bad it was."

BABY FARMING

"Baby farming was a business carried out throughout the country," said historian Ken Wells. "If a mother was unable to look after their child, there was an option of sending them out to a baby farmer, also known as fostering, with the understanding that they could visit the child whenever they wanted to."

On the surface they were providing a service to a growing need. They took an unwanted child and gave them to a foster parent. Only those foster parents and caregivers didn't always have the best interests of the infant at heart.

"MOTHER'S FRIEND"

The majority of these "caregivers" resorted to starving out the babies. They sedated crying babies with alcohol or drugs usually using Godfrey's Cordial, also known as 'Mother's Friend'. This syrup was one of the most popular medicines given to infants and children in both the United States and England in the latter years of the 18th and early 19th centuries. The syrup was used as a panacea to everything from colic to jaundice to excessive crying to diarrhea. 'Mother's Friend' was harmful despite its harmless sounding name as it contained one grain of opium for every two ounces. Many infants were poisoned from this syrup which was administered in secret by nurses who wanted to keep babies under their care in a deep state of sleep and thus more manageable.

"A hungry child, a noisy child, is a difficult child to raise," author Allison Vale said. "And something that was chillingly referred to colloquially as 'the Quietness' was an over the counter anti-colic cordial and it did contain liquid opium which was laudanum and in some cases brandy."

"People gave babies laudanum when they were supposed to be giving them food," Klansman said. "Because it dulled the need, or dulled the awareness of the baby that it was hungry. Of course it didn't nourish the baby so eventually a baby that was given that and not given enough food would die."

The babies would die from severe malnutrition but the coroner would record the death as "debility from birth", "lack of breast milk" or "starvation."

There were those guilt-ridden mothers who returned to the baby-farming homes to check on their children but would find their efforts blocked. Most would be too scared or embarrassed to inform the police of any wrongdoing. The police themselves had numerous problems tracking any children that were deemed missing.

"Dead infants," Vale said. "Or abandoned infants were as commonplace in British cities as roadkill today. Babies were found parceled up in railroad stations, under railroad arches."

"It was desperation," McCormick added. "For the vast majority of these ladies."

TO A MANNER BORN

With Dane's departure to the States, Amelia set her sights on taking her place in the baby-farming business. She had just given birth to her own daughter, Ellen, but in 1869 her husband George died.

A widow at age 32 with a baby, Amelia needed a new source of income...

She began taking in pregnant women as she placed ads to nurse and adopt the babies. In return, she required a large one-time fee and clothing for the child. She began meeting with expectant young women, convincing them that she was someone who could be trusted in providing a safe and loving home for their child.

Before she followed through with her plan, however, she put her own child up for adoption and sent her away.

"It was a choice that she made," Vale said. "She had options. She could have worked through. But instead what she does is to farm her own child out and opt for the easy money that she seemed to be able to make."

"As Amelia chose to go into the baby farming business," Rattle said. "She was maybe able to travel around here, there and everywhere adopting babies so it made sense for her daughter to be out of the way."

Three years after her first husband George died, Amelia remarried. His name was William Dyer, a brewers laborer from Bristol. They had two children together, Mary Ann aka Polly and William Samuel.

Amelia eventually left William, however, as the latter lost his job and offered little in the way of finances.

Strapped for cash, Amelia decided to dispense with the heavy cost of letting the babies die through neglect and starvation. So after each child was born she promptly murdered them, thus incurring a windfall of profits.

"Baby farmers used different methods," Klansman said. "Some of which are less palatable than others."

"Quite often she would suffocate babies at birth," Rattle said. "Smothering the baby the moment its head came out, before it turned blue as that would be a sign that it had taken its first breath. (She made) it would look like a stillbirth so the death certificate would all be above board."

When her daughter Polly asked why so many babies came and disappeared, Amelia described herself as the "angel maker."

"I'm sending little children to Jesus," Amelia said. "Because he wanted them far more than their mothers did."

"Cold," Alan McCormick of New Scotland Yard said in describing Amelia. "Those kids meant nothing to her. It was just a means of getting money."

It can be argued, however, that once Amelia got a taste of killing she did it more for the power than the money and greed.

"The actual killing of the child," Holmes said. "Watching the child peacefully to some degree die. It parallels perhaps seeing her mother pass away where she felt an almost God-like power over these children that she had decided were going to go to their maker."

AROUSING SUSPICION

"Amelia was already aware of the fact that this was not going to be about her helping children," forensic psychologist David Holmes said. "This was going to be a fairly cruel and anti-mothering act that would be carried out in order to gain all of this money."

Amelia successfully avoided police involvement until 1879, a good ten years into her murderous ways. A doctor became suspicious about the number of child deaths he had been called in to certify under Amelia's care.

"The inquests were held in Somerset," Vale said. "And they're (the police) pretty certain that the babies have died as a direct result of neglect and opium overdose. But they can't prove it. And interestingly, she gets off with a six months sentence with hard labor."

Without a coroner that was able to rule completely against her, Amelia would have undoubtedly been executed by hanging.

"Its incredibly really," Rattle said. "That she only got six months. And there was one example, we read of a chap who got twelve months for stealing a piece of bacon."

Amelia took the punishment hard, becoming an emotional wreck during her jail stay. She resumed her business, however, as soon as she was released.

"In the long term," Holmes reasoned. "It mostly would have served as a very hard lesson in forensic awareness that she wasn't gonna get caught again. And there was no way she was going to leave any evidence which had been the problem in leading up to her capture."

She was sent to mental hospitals for supposed mental illness and suicidal ideations but these seemed to be well-timed acts. From her experience of working in an asylum, Amelia knew the tricks of the trade in order to make her stay an easy one.

"I don't think Amelia Dyer was insane," said Vale. "I think she was a very bad person who deliberately committed murder for profit."

Amelia had both an alcohol and substance abuse problem, using on a regular basis as she began her killings once again.

"Certainly the drugs would have had an impact on her," Richards said. "On her mental state. Maybe induced this complete detachment from reality."

"A long term laudanum habit," Vale concurred. "Will lead to periods of depression. It can lead to mood swings even when you're not under the influence. I think it also exacerbates any underlying mental health issues."

RETURNING TO BABY FARMING

In 1884, British society took a much harder line against baby farming and any sign of neglect or abuse would be reported.

"She definitely changes her modus operandi at this point (after 1884)," Vale said. "She's beginning to murder these children."

In 1890, Amelia took on the care of the illegitimate baby of a governess. She had begun targeting the babies of the more affluent because of the larger amounts of money involved. The higher up the social class the woman was, however, the more risk was involved as the woman may have means to question and come after Amelia.

"This was a young governess who fell in love with the young master of the house that she worked in and had got pregnant," Rattle said. "She was left on her own and she responds to an advert, gets in touch with Amelia Dyer and moves in with her. Amelia was able to gain the trust of this woman as with many others, so much so that the governess was persuaded to leave her baby in the care of Amelia once it was born."

The governess, however, returned to visit her baby months later and immediately became suspicious that the child she was given was not hers. She stripped the baby to see if a birth mark was present on one of its hips. It wasn't and the governess immediately informed the authorities.

The police, however, could never pin Amelia down.

"She managed to put them off time and time again by sending them on wild goose chases," Rattle said. "She said she had sent them to a couple that moved here...that moved there."

Amelia continued to move from town to town but still found herself being stalked by the governess who wouldn't give up.

"She did feel hounded," Richards said. "I'm sure that would have had an impact on her. She would have felt that pressure."

Amelia then feigned another nervous breakdown and a doctor was brought in. "The birds are telling me to do it! The birds are telling me to do it!" she would cry out, forcing the doctor to send her to an asylum.

"She was a very clever lady," Holmes said. "With the police getting close to her and she needed to lose herself and what better place to go than somewhere like that (a mental asylum)."

Her mental illness continued on unabated as she drank two bottles of laudanum in an attempted suicide. Her long term use of opium, however, allowed her to build up the tolerance necessary to survive.

"Amelia would be drawn to the idea of self-medicating," Holmes said. "Possibly seeing it as a route, a means to ease the situation, make it even easier for her to put up with what she was doing."

"She took it (opium) on a regular basis," Richards said. "She took it almost daily so she was an addict. So that would induce a form of state from her mentally where she would be detached from reality and I think that was part of her coping mechanism to detach from the reality of what she was doing."

After that close call and subsequent hospital release, Amelia resumed baby farming and murder.

"Her mental breakdowns were very short lived," Richards noted. "She would be out of sorts for a period of time that get it all back together again. To me that would say there isn't a mental illness there."

A CLEVER KILLER

She wised up to doing things on the books and decided to stop getting doctors to issue death certificates. Amelia decided to kill and bury the bodies herself. In order to do this, she would have to be a killer on the run as inevitably the mothers would come back seeking to reclaim their children or check on their welfare. Amelia took her family to different cities to escape suspicion as soon as things got too hot. She would use a series of different aliases and rename her businesses.

"Amelia committed what many serial killers do," Holmes explained. "The mistake of accelerating and being over enthusiastic. Either for reasons that she was enjoying the process or quite simply greed was driving her over the edge."

Baby farming began to gain the attention and compassion of the British ruling class, however. They asked why if they had laws for the prevention of the cruelty of animals then why didn't there laws protecting children. With the arrest and hanging of Margaret Waters (another baby farming killer) and the fleeing Dyer, Amelia's colleagues were going downhill fast and perhaps she thought her time was limited.

By 1893, Amelia had another breakdown but was released from the Wells mental asylum. This would be the last time she would be hospitalized. She moved to Caversham, Berkshire with a woman named Jane "Granny" Smith who didn't know of Amelia's exploits.

"She befriends an old lady named Jane Smith," Vale said. "She's widowed and resigned to spend her last days in the workhouse. Amelia seduces her with stories of rescuing the unwanted infants. Of nursing them. And it's a very, very seductive image. And Jane Smith buys into it, wholesale."

Her daughter Mary Ann aka Polly and her husband Arthur Palmer came along as well.

The group moved to 45 Kensington Road, Reading Berkshire in that same year. Amelia had the perfect front. She coached Jane Smith to call her "mother" in front of prospective clients while Amelia would call her "Granny."

A ruse to project a mother-daughter image and put the guards down of the pregnant young women.

"Jane Smith didn't get the life she was promised at all," Rattle said. "She was treated as no more than a servant really. She was made to look after the children, to clean the house."

Amelia then puts her adoptions into overdrive. The babies come in and out of the house with such rapidity that old lady Jane Smith doesn't even learn their names.

Eyewitnesses later claimed that there were six infants a day coming to and from the house daily.

THE MURDERS CONTINUE

The advertisement in the "Miscellaneous" column of the Bristol Times & Mirror newspaper was poignant.

In January of 1896 a popular barmaid named Evelina Marmon gave birth to a daughter out of wedlock. She named the baby Doris and she sought immediately to have it adopted. She placed an ad in the "Miscellaneous" section of the Bristol Times & Mirror newspaper.

*"Wanted, respectable woman to take young child."* Marmon intended to go back to work and hoped to eventually reclaim her child.

Evelina was a God-fearing farmer's daughter who left the farm for city life. She found work as a barmaid in the saloon of the Plough

Hotel, an old coaching inn. She was buxom with blonde hair and had a vibrant personality. She had plenty of suitors and became pregnant by one of the male patrons who left her deserted.

Evelina knew she could not bring up the baby on her own.

She would have to find a foster home for little Doris - to have her "adopted out", in the language of the time - go back to work and hope in time to be able to reclaim her child.

Next to her own ad was an advertisement that read *"Married couple with no family would adopt healthy child, nice country home. Terms, £10".*

Marmon answered the ad which was addressed to a "Mrs. Harding", an alias of Amelia. A few days later Amelia wrote back, saying *"I should be glad to have a dear little baby girl, one I could bring up and call my own. We are plain, homely people, in fairly good circumstances. I don't want a child for money's sake, but for company and home comfort... Myself and my husband are dearly fond of children. I have no child of my own. A child with me will have a good home and a mother's love. It is just lovely here, heatlhy and pleasant. There is an orchard opposite our front door."*

Evelina was assured that she could visit whenever she wished.

*"Rest assured I will do my duty by that dear child. I will be a mother, as far as lies in my power."*

*"It is just lovely here, healthy and pleasant. There is an orchard opposite our front door."*

Evelina tried to negotiate a weekly fee for the care of Doris but Amelia wanted a substantial one-time fee to be paid upfront. Evelina, seemingly with no other choice, agreed to pay the £10, and a week later "Mrs Harding" arrived in Cheltenham.

Evelina was surprised that Amelia aka "Mrs. Harding" was old (59 years) and heavy set (over 210 lbs). She remained reluctant at first but gave in as the elderly woman immediately showed her Doris some affection, covering her with a shawl.

Evelina gave the old lady a cardboard box of clothes she had prepared – nappies, chemises, petticoats, frocks, nightgowns, and a powder box. She also enclosed the money and received a signed receipt from "Mrs.Harding."

She accompanied her baby daughter and her eventual killer to Cheltenham station then on to Gloucester. Evelina stood there crying through the hot steam on the platform as the 5:20 p.m train took her baby away.

When Evelina returned home, she described herself as "a broken woman."

Days later, she received a letter from "Mrs. Harding" offering her assurance that all was well with her daughter. Evelina wrote back but received no replies afterward.

Amelia told Evelina that she would be going to Reading but lied. She traveled to 76 Mayo Road, Willesden, London where her daughter Mary Ann was staying. Amelia then took some white edging tape and wrapped it around the baby's neck, making a strangling knot. The baby did not die immediately.

"I used to like to watch them with the tape around their neck," Amanda said. "But it was soon all over with them."

"The idea of strangling and using the tape may make it seem almost symbolical or bizarre to ourselves," Holmes said. "But in terms of criminal awareness she was aware of the fact that if she tried to suffocate a baby its not always absolutely certain that the baby is dead."

The mother and daughter team wrapped the baby up with a napkin. They kept the clothes that Evelina gave her and hoped to sell it to a pawnbroker. Amelia used some of the money to pay the rent to her landlady and gave the woman a pair of child's boots as a present for her own little girl.

The following day, April 1st of 1896, a young boy named Harry Simmons was taken to the Mayo Road residence. Amelia had no spare white edging tape available and used the tape from Doris' corpse to strangle the year old boy.

The next day both bodies were rolled into a carpet bag, their corpses stacked one on top of the other. Bricks were added inside for additional weight. Amelia headed back toward Reading, taking the bus to Paddington and then the train. She dragged the carpet bag through the streets until she reached the River Thames. She had a secluded spot at Caversham Lock and she forced the carpet bag through the railing and didn't leave until she heard it splash into the waters below.

She didn't know she had a witness as a man passed, hurrying on his way home calling out "Good night."

A SHOCKING DISCOVERY

Ironically, only days before the dumping of the bodies a package was fished out of the Thames by a bargeman. This package was the work of Amelia as she had not weighed it down adequately. It contained the body of a baby girl named Helena Fry. With only a small police force available in Reading, a Constable Anderson made a significant discovery. He found a label from Temple Meads Station, Bristol and he used microscopic analysis of the wrapping paper. He found a faintly legible name. A "Mrs.Thomas" and an address.

The address of Amelia Dyer.

The police immediately placed Amelia's home under surveillance. They did enough research on Amelia and knew that she would "disappear" if she thought she was under suspicion. So they decided they would be better served if they would use a young woman as a decoy to secure a meeting with Amelia and discuss the prospect of using her "adoptive services."

On April 3$^{rd}$, while Amelia was waiting on the decoy to arrive, she answered the door to a police raid. The smell of decomposing bodies radiated throughout her home but no human remains were found. The police found other evidence, however, such as the white edging tape, telegrams describing adoption arrangements, pawn tickets for children's clothing, receipts for newspaper ads and letters from distraught mothers asking about the welfare of their child.

The police determined that in the few months Amelia had been in Reading at least twenty children had been placed into her care. She had been preparing to move again, this time to the town of Somerset.

Amelia was arrested on April 4th, three days after the murders of Doris Marmon and Harry Simmons. The Thames River was searched and six more bodies were discovered, including Doris and Harry.

Each child had been strangled with the seamstress white tape and Amelia later told police that "was how you could tell it was one of mine."

Eleven days later, Evelina Marmon had been contacted by police as they found her name in items found in Amelia's home. Distraught, she came to identify her daughter's remains.

THE TRIAL OF A KILLER

An inquest was held a month later. Amelia's daughter Mary Ann and her husband Arthur were not charged as there was no direct evidence that they were her accomplices. Arthur was set free because of a confession handwritten by Amelia. She wrote:

*Sir will you kindly grant me the favour of presenting this to the magistrates on Saturday the 18th instant I have made this statement out, for I may not have the opportunity then I must relieve my mind I do know and I feel my days are numbered on this earth but I do feel it is an awful thing drawing innocent people into trouble I do know I shal have to answer before my Maker in Heaven for the awful crimes I have committed but as God Almighty is my judge in Heaven a on Hearth neither my daughter Mary Ann Palmer nor her husband Alfred Ernest Palmer I do most solemnly declare neither of them had any thing at all to do with it, they never knew I contemplated doing such a wicked thing until it was to late I am speaking the truth and nothing but the truth as I hope to be forgiven, I myself and I alone must stand before my Maker in Heaven to give an answer for it all witnes my hand*

*Amelia Dyer.*

*—April 16, 1896*

On May 22<sup>nd</sup>, 1896, Amelia appeared in court and pleaded guilty to the murder of Doris Marmon. Her family and friends testified that they had their own suspicions about Amelia and spoke of times that she evaded discovery. A man came forth claiming he had seen and spoken to Amelia as she had disposed of two bodies at Caversham Lock proved key to the prosecution.

Amelia used insanity as a defense, offering her stays in mental asylums as proof of her instability. The prosecution, however, argued that her symptoms were well-rehearsed actions to avoid suspicion as both of her hospital stays coincided with times that Amelia felt her murders would be discovered.

The jury took four and a half minutes to find her guilty. Amelia then spent three weeks in her condemned cell, filling five journals with her confessions. A chaplain visited her the night before her execution and asked if she had anything to confess. She offered him her journals, asking "isn't this enough?"

Amelia was then subpoenaed to appear as a witness in her daughter's own trial for murder which was set for a week after her own execution date. The court ruled, however, that Amelia became "legally dead" after she was sentenced and her testimony would be inadmissible.

On the day of her execution, Amelia discovered that the charges against her daughter had been dropped.

On June 10<sup>th</sup>, 1896, Amelia Dyer was hanged by James Billington at Newgate Prison. Asked on the scaffold if she had anything to say, she said "I have nothing to say."

URBAN LEGEND?

It remains unknown as to why Amelia's daughter Mary Ann aka Polly was never convicted. Her own daughter provided the majority of the testimony that procured the conviction of her mother but nothing is said about her own involvement.

And the baby murders did not stop after Amelia's death.

Two years after her execution, railroad workers inspecting carriages found a parcel tied up with a string inside a siding on the Plymouth express.

Inside was a three-week old baby girl. The infant was shivering and wet...but alive.

A little research showed that the baby was the child of a widow named Jane Hill. Hill had given the baby to a woman named "Mrs. Stewart" for the one time fee of £12.

"The little one would have a good home and a parent's love and care," Mrs. Stewart had written, her prose eerily echoing that of Amelia Dyer. "Mrs. Stewart" had picked up the baby at Plymouth and dumped her on the next train.

The conjecture was that "Mrs. Stewart" was none other than Polly, Amelia's daughter.

# BABY KILLER : THE TRUE STORY OF CHRISTINA MARIE RIGGS

DIANE ULLMER

Christina Riggs had all the drugs she needed.

She had filled her prescription for the anti-depressant Elavil at the pharmacy. She had stolen morphine and potassium chloride from the hospital. Now all she had to do was follow through.

"Kids," she bellowed out from the living room table. "Vitamins!"

The two sleepy-eyed children emerged from their bedroom. Christina gave them a small amount of Elavil, dropping the pill in their mouth and watching them drink it down with a cup of water.

A few minutes later, she carried them both back to bed.

Looking down at her two young children, she began to sob.

Shelby, just two years old, in her pink jumper. Justin, five years old, in his white pajamas with battleship designs.

I have to do this. Things will only get worse for them.

THE GREATEST TABOO

Christina Marie Riggs was twenty-six years when she decided to kill her children.

"A mother is supposed to protect her own children," Riggs' Defense Attorney John Wesley Hall Jr. said. "And here she didn't and it doesn't make sense. Two defenseless children that didn't know what was coming."

After Christina sedated her children, she proceeded with her plan of injecting them with potassium chloride. She knew that the drug was administered for lethal injection executions and would stop the heart within minutes.

What she didn't know was that the drug had to be administered in a diluted form. If it is injected without any dilution, it will burn through the skin then burst through the vein.

Ignorant of the consequences, Christina injected the lethal cocktail into her son Justin first.

She wanted a painless death. She did not want her children to go through life suffering like she did.

But then her son woke up screaming.

The potassium chloride she injected was binding and burning through his blood vessel linings.

He cried and cried and wouldn't stop.

Christina began crying herself...

CHILDHOOD TRAUMA

Christina Riggs had a troubled childhood growing up in Oklahoma City, OK.

She was separated from her brothers and sisters after her parent's divorce. Raised alone by her mother, she detailed in a prison diary sexual abuses that took place in her childhood.

She wrote how her stepbrother sexually abusing her from the age of seven to thirteen. At the age of thirteen, she was molested by a neighbor as well.

By the time she entered her teenage years, Christina was obese, using food as an emotional outlet. She also began abusing alcohol and marijuana.

"She indulged in overeating because she didn't want to appear attractive," forensic psychologist Paula Orange said. "That behavior was part of a psychological response to being molested. 'If I become fat and ugly then he won't want me anymore.' No one will bother me, no one will hurt me."

In her teenage years, however, Christina began to use sex as a way to get what she wanted, which was love.

"It isn't uncommon for abused young women to become very promiscuous," Orange said. "It is learned behavior. She became defective, if you will, and should have gotten help. Unfortunately, this is not a good recipe for someone who wants to have a healthy stable relationship and raise children."

"I felt that no boy liked me because of my weight," Christina wrote in her journal. "So I became sexually promiscuous because I thought that was the only way I could have a boyfriend."

She became pregnant by the age of sixteen but gave the baby boy up for adoption.

After high school, Christina went to a vocational school to become a licensed practical nurse (LPN). She obtained employment as a home care nurse and then later worked full-time at a VA hospital.

Her dating life remained steady albeit unsuccessful. She went from one man to the next, dating a Navy ensign named Jon Riggs and a bouncer before meeting Timothy Thompson. Thompson was an Air Force private at Tinker Air Force Base.

Three years after her first child, Christina would become pregnant with Timothy's baby. She informed Timothy her pregnancy the day before he was to be discharged from the Air Force.

Timothy, however, did not take the news well. He would not accept responsibility and moved back to his native Minnesota.

"Chrissy's luck with men was about zero to nothing," Carol Thomas, Christina's mother said.

But while her relationship ended with Timothy, Christina hooked back up with Jon Riggs who returned home after being on leave with the Navy.

"It was great," Christina wrote. "He felt the baby's first kick. As far as he was concerned, it was his baby."

Justin Thomas was born on June 7th, 1992.

"As I held Justin in my arms and looked into his little face, I became so scared," Christina wrote. "Would I be a good Mom? Could I give him all he needed?"

Riggs would move in with Christina and the two hoped for the best. Christina would become pregnant again and the couple would marry in July of 1993.

But misfortune would strike again as Christina would suffer a miscarriage on her wedding night.

The marriage would go south from there as Christina alternated between being depressed to having suicidal thoughts. She blamed her mental state on her birth control medication and a doctor gave her the anti-depressant Prozac.

The medication worked for a while but then Christina inexplicably stopped taking the drug. She kept her sadness to herself and didn't want to burden others with her problems.

"She's always been that way," Christina's mother said. "If I pushed her hard she might get mad and tell me what was going on."

By 1994, Christina would become pregnant and deliver a healthy baby girl in December named Shelby. This would mark the high point of Christina's life as "Sissie" and "Bubbie", the two nicknames for her children, brought immeasurable joy into her life.

She would write that it was the happiest time of her life as both she and Jon cried when they held their new baby in their arms. Things were happy for once in her life.

Christina continued to work as a vocational nurse and was assigned to work at a triage station which served to help the victims of the Oklahoma City Federal Building terrorist bombing. She would suffer post-traumatic stress disorder as a result. Later at her trial, the prosecuting attorneys would argue that the hospital had no record of Christina serving after the bombing. This may be nitpicking as authorities were lenient with record keeping during that urgent situation.

STRESS AND STRAIN

A year later, the couple would move to Sherwood, Arkansas to be closer to Christina's mother, Carole.

Carole worked as a food service worker at Baptist Hospital and Christina was able to find a job there as well, once again working as a licensed practical nurse.

The children go on to have ailments that would stress out the already fragile Christina. Shelby would have chronic ear infections that made doctor visits a routine thing. Justin was diagnosed with attention deficit disorder and his hyper nature would grate on the nerves of his parents.

Financial difficulties and the stress of running a family would put a strain on the marriage and the couple would eventually divorce. Her husband, Jon Riggs, had a volatile temper that he eventually took out on the young Justin. Jon would punch Justin in the abdomen with such force that the young boy had to go to the emergency room.

Jon would then abandon the family.

"Justin would say, 'My Daddy hurt me, and then he went away,' " Christina's mother recalled.

Christina would receive limited child support from Jon and had to work long hours to provide for her family. The more hours she worked, the more she had to pay for daycare which proved to be a daily traumatic event.

Shelby would cry as Christina would leave her at the facility.

"She was beating on the glass, yelling, 'Mama! Mama!' " Christina recalled.

Despite her increased efforts, Christina could not get ahead financially. She began writing bad checks. Bills remained unpaid. Car insurance. Car registration. Lights and utilities.

"I started out in a boat with a small hole," Christina said. "But the hole kept getting bigger, and no matter how hard you bail, you keep sinking. I was tired and I gave up. Suicide seemed like the only thing."

## A HISTORY OF MENTAL ILLNESS

Christina had a cousin that killed herself. Her mother had also tried to kill herself when Christina was a baby. Her grandmother was committed to a mental institution.

But Christina would outdo them all in one fateful night.

"Just speaking in general," Orange said. "When mothers kill their children they do not poison them. In the case of Christina, she was applying what she thought would be a lethal injection."

But even with a history of mental illness in the family, nobody could have predicted how the sweet and caring Christina could commit such a heinous crime.

"Chrissy always wanted to help people," Christina's sister, Elizabeth Nottingham said. "She was always helping someone."

But Nottingham had some valuable psychological insight on her sister. She was a mental health counselor and had been close to Christina.

She wanted to know what drove her sister to kill her own children. After her sister's arrest, she began fishing around her house, looking for some kind of clue, a sign that everyone had missed.

"I was almost hoping to find that she wasn't a good parent," Nottingham said. "Then I could be mad at her. You know, I went through her house with a fine toothed comb. All the chemicals were locked away. The food was in the refrigerator. Even pictures of their fathers was in their room above each of their beds. She was great with the kids."

## MORE TROUBLE WITH MEN

What Christina's sister would find out was that she simply could not find a decent man. That one relationship where everything would be ideal.

After her divorce from Jon, Christina would enter into another relationship which again would not go well.

"The guy didn't just break her heart," Nottingham said. "But took her credit card. I mean, it's one thing to have someone dump you, it's another to have someone rip you off and leave you destitute too."

After this break-up, Christina would sit at her dining room table both broke and broken-hearted. She had no man in her life. She had no means to pay her family's bills.

Seeing only dark lights ahead, Christina would lapse into a deep depression. She went to her doctor again who prescribed her more Prozac which used irregularly.

"She may have stopped taking the Prozac when she killed the babies," Orange said. "When someone just stops that medication cold-turkey it can have some side effects like increased irritability, irrational mood changes, and an even deeper depression."

"So she had the perfect storm brewing," Nottingham said. "She had depression, she had all of these personal failures. You know, people talk about having rainy days and Mondays. And in fact 'Rainy days and Mondays' was the CD that was in her CD player."

BACK TO THAT FATEFUL NIGHT

Christina had to kill herself. Her emotional bank account had been overdrawn for years.

But she couldn't stand the thought of leaving her children alone.

"If she left the kids behind," Hall Jnr said. "She was afraid that the children would be separated, go to their father's, for instance, and be split up."

"She just thought there was no other way out," Nottingham said. "She thought that no one else would take care of her kids. And that they would be better off, in her mind, she was saving them from future sadness."

With Justin screaming in pain, Christina panicked. She began sobbing but whatever remain of her maternal instinct kicked in and she tried to inject him with morphine.

Toxicology reports didn't reveal whether or not she did this.

But what she did do was suffocate her young son with a pillow. Sobbing, she then did the same deed to her baby daughter, Shelby.

Shaking with adrenaline and grief, Christina wobbled on shaky legs back to her living room. She took out her bottle of Elavil, an anti-depressant, and swallowed the remaining twenty-eight pills. Her nerves calming, she tried injecting the potassium chloride into her own arm.

The chemical burn right through her vein, collapsing it.

The drugs began taking effect and Christina fainted to the floor, hoping her nightmare would finally end.

THE DAY AFTER

The lethal mixture had burned a half-inch hole into Christina's arm. She didn't show up for work the next day and her mother called her cell phone and land line repeatedly.

Worried that she received no response, Carole drove to Christina's apartment and let herself in.

To her horror, she thought everyone was dead, including Christina.

"All I could do was turn around and around and scream and holler, 'No. No. No.' There's no way to describe how I felt."

Frantic, she called 911 and yelling into the phone, "My daughter and babies are dead."

Paramedics would arrive.

The children were dead.

But the medics were able to resuscitate Christina. She was transported to the intensive care unit and was kept under guard by the police.

"I had to do it so I wouldn't leave them behind," Christina was overheard saying in her hospital room. The treating physician, Dr. Jim

Rice, would later testify that Christina as "combative at times" and "just incoherent and not really making any sense."

As soon as Christina became reasonably coherent, she was taken to the police station for booking.

THE INTERROGATION

On November 6th, 1997, Christina was interrogated by a Detective Jones and Detective Sharon Williams.

"Christina, what we are doing is investigating the death of your two babies. Do you want to tell us what happened?" Jones asked.

"I killed them," Christina said, crying.

"What did you say?"

"I said-"

"Did you say you killed them?"

"I'm sorry."

"How did you go about doing that?" Jones asked.

"I got some bottles and stuff from here...I need a cigarette...Darvocet."

"Are you saying that you got some medicine from the hospital?"

Christina nodded.

"Christina, how did you do it? Did you give them an injection? Did you give them a shot?"

"I tried to ... and ... I did it with Justin because I figured with him being the oldest one that he would give me more problems. So, I tried it with him and I thought it would just stop his heart. But it hurt. Oh, he said it hurt ...It didn't work, he just kept calling, 'Momma! Momma! Momma!' I just figured it was too late now because I had no place to turn back to. I cleaned out my checking account and gave my mother all the money I had."

"Christina, why did you do this?" Jones asked.

"Because I wanted to die," Christina said, crying again. "But I didn't want to die and leave my kids behind or for them to be a burden to somebody else. I didn't want them to think I didn't love them and I didn't want them to grow up separately because they have two different Daddies. And I knew if I passed away they would be fighting my Mother for custody and I didn't want that for nobody."

"You felt like you were doing it for the kids' sake?"

"In a way, yeah... my piece of mind."

"Christina, did you really want to die?"

Christina didn't respond. She continued crying.

"And you felt it would be better if your children just die with you and ... were the children already dead before you took your medicine?"

"Yes."

"How long had they been dead before you took your medicine?"

"About twenty minutes."

"About twenty minutes?"

"That's because I drank and got up and smoked a cigarette and got back and sit for a minute and...I was like, 'Okay, I'm going to do it now. I can't turn back now because you've already killed Justin.' And ... so I did it."

"What time did you give them the medicine? Do you remember?"

"Justin about 10:15 or 10:30."

"10:15 or 10:30 in the morning?"

"No, in the evening."

"Oh, in the evening?"

"Last night."

"Okay."

"Then I smoked another cigarette and waited," Christina paused. "And suffocated Shelby."

"You suffocated Shelby? What did ... how did you suffocate her?"

"I put a pillow over her head."

"Okay, Did you ... Had you given her any medicine at all, or ... any of the Morphine or the Potassium Chloride?"

"I slipped them … I made them drink half of an Elavil because I figured that would make them sleep a little bit better so that it wouldn't wake them."

"So, Shelby, you killed her with a pillow. You suffocated her. And what about the little boy. How did you do him?"

"I gave him the medicine and when it didn't work."

"You suffocated him too?"

"Yes."

"With a pillow? Were they fighting while you suffocated them?"

"Justin did. Shelby a little bit but not much," Christina began to cry again.

"When did you decide to do this, Christina? On what day did you decide to do this?"

"Uh … the best I remember it was Sunday night or Saturday night because we was out talking and this and that and the other … and they caught me."

"Who caught you?"

"I was depressed. I was thinking about what was going on in my life and that things aren't always working for me and…"

"When did you get those drugs from the hospital?"

"When? Yesterday."

"Yesterday? You mean the day that you killed them? Is that the day that you got the drugs? The last was it … "

"Was it the last day that you worked at the hospital or the day before that? "I think …"

"When you got … "

"I got the drugs and I gave them to my kids. That's the only drugs that I had in my hand. And I know that there was three Valiums in a vial in there, but there wasn't enough to even cover the jar up and put it in my pocket and bring them home. And I know I should have thought better … had somebody rinsing with me, but … they were just what came home in my pockets."

"Did you know what you were going to do when you took the drugs from the hospital? Did you have intentions of giving them to your children? And how many days did you think about this before you killed your children?"

"About three weeks. Two weeks."

"Two or three weeks. In other words, you've been thinking about doing this for the last two or three weeks? What made you decide to just go ahead and do it?"

"I just can't take it no more."

"You couldn't take it anymore."

"I felt like I was out of control," Christina said.

"Did you just feel like your life was in a mess? Had you talked to anybody about this? Your Mom or anybody?"

"I've tried to talk to people about what I feel and what I think and they were just like, 'I don't have time right now. We'll do it some other time.' So, I just got to where I don't care anymore. I tried but they can't give me no help."

"So you just felt like nobody was listening to you? Okay, Christina ...Christina, do you have anything more to say about your babies or anything? "I wish I hadn't done it now."

Christina would then go on an incoherent ramble, explaining how she saw her mother riding down an escalator with a bunch of old people. The detectives, however, got the damning evidence they needed and ended the interrogation.

PRISON AND JAIL

Christina would find a hostile environment in prison. The majority of her fellow prisoners were women who were taken away from their children by force. They had contempt for Christina's crime.

One inmate spat in her face and her life was threatened.

Christina was then moved to an isolated cell where she remained until her trial.

She would be charged with two counts of first-degree murder which was punishable by death in the state of Arkansas.

"We tried to show that she was under extreme emotional disturbance," Hall Jr said. "To justify either not imposing the death penalty or hopefully finding her guilty of second-degree murder."

"I just hope that out of all her misery," Nottingham said. "The sadness of our family. That we can shed some light on the causes of this for other people and that maybe they'll be able to look at the symptoms and look at the situations and maybe intervene for someone else."

But the prosecuting attorney, as well as the community, believed that Christina was guilty of performing a selfish act, an act wherein she tried to free herself from motherhood.

The most damning evidence at the trial, aside from the interrogation tapes, would be the account of the physicians.

One doctor would testify that it would take three to six minutes to suffocate someone to death. Because of that time period, the jurors would be able to envision how Christina commit a willful act of murder. Christina had, in essence, a struggling toddler under her pillow for about three to six minutes...suffocating to death.

"They just wanted her to be evil," Nottingham said of the prosecuting attorney's intent. "It was easier that way."

"Essentially, what the jury saw was that she was self-centered," argued Pulaski Prosecuting Attorney Larry Jegley. "That she viewed the children as an inconvenience and an interference with what she wanted to pursue. She placed her interests above those of the children."

Jegley argued that Christina was a self-centered and premeditated murderer. He brought up the fact that she had locked the children up in the house (according to a neighbor) in order that she could go out to a Karaoke party. He urged the jury not to buy into her manipulation to feel sorry for her. "There were lots of people who have it worse than she did."

The jury would side with the prosecution and find Christina guilty after a very short deliberation period.

THE IRONY

Christina Riggs would be sentenced to death by lethal injection via potassium chloride...The same method that she used to try to kill her children and herself.

"It was a cruel irony that they finished what she started," Hall Jr said. "Almost the exact same way except she was strapped down to a table."

Christina would appeal the sentencing but did so with reluctance. She wanted to die.

"I'll be with my children and with God," Christina said. "I'll be where there's no more pain. Maybe I'll find some peace."

Her defense attorney John Wesley Hall Jr was allowed to witness the execution.

"You can see their face," Hall Jr said. "It allows them to say their last words. The face changes color as the drugs take effect. You turn gray. The skin turns gray. And it's rather shocking to watch it happen."

"She was so depressed that it became this black sheet over her eyes that she couldn't see through," Orange said. "She wanted to spare her own children from the kind of life that she had. She had lost complete hope and really over thought things. That's how her depression warped her. It warped her enough to think that she was doing her children a favor by killing them."

Christina was sent to death row and was haunted by the memories of her children. She openly stated that she tried "not to think about them" because when she did it was like someone "ripping them away from her all over again."

"A lot of regret," Christina said. "That's what goes through my mind, day-in, day-out. God's punishing me. He let me live so I would suffer."

Riggs was flown in from McPherson Jail to Cummins in order to prep for her execution. She would be administered the lethal injection at 9:28 PM CDT on May 2nd, 2000.

"No words can express just how sorry I am for taking the lives of my babies," Riggs said in a prepared statement. "No way I can make up for or take away the pain I have caused everyone who knew and loved them. I love you, my babies."

# BLACK WIDOW BETTY LOU BEETS

ALICE WATERS

Betty Lou Beets is a perfect historical example of how multifaceted crime can be, how a victim could become an aggressor, or an aggressor may adopt the mask of victimhood, and how all is not necessarily as it seems. Convicted for murdering two men and assaulting or attempting to kill four, Betty Lou's story is one that would send chills down the spine of any man from any era. Only the fourth woman to be executed for murder, despite the overall statistics hovering around forty to fifty cases of capital punishment per year, her crimes were too gruesome and cold for the court to offer her a lesser sentence... or were they? As we shall see when we delve into her history, despite Betty Lou's extensive criminal record and constant charges against her from ex husbands and her own children, the justice system was eager to give her a way out of the death sentence and allow her to live her natural life out in prison. And although there were some mitigating circumstances, it is telling that Betty Lou Beets almost got away with a life sentence in a situation where many others would have been executed without remorse.

Betty Lou Beets was born Betty Lou Dunevant on the 12th of March 1937, in Roxboro, North Carolina, USA. Her parents were initially tobacco farmers, whose main pleasure in life was alcohol, resulting in rampant alcoholism and a violent family life not atypical of the rural poor of the Great Depression. They lived on a diet of salt pork and various flours, barely touching vegetables or fruit, let alone eggs, fish, nuts or pulses, essential for developing a healthy brain and body. Furthermore, Betty Lou was disabled. She was not completely deaf, but hard of hearing due to having contracted the measles some time between the ages of three and six. Her fever was so severe and prolonged that she suffered damage to her brain and ears. As her hearing was affected at such a young age, she suffered an impairment to her speech similar to what many deaf or hard of hearing children suffer. At another time, or in another family, Betty Lou may have received treatment and hearing aids, but as a poor family in 1940, they could not afford to get her the treatment she would have needed to hear and speak normally. Her education was strongly impacted as she could not learn to read or study, resulting in borderline illiteracy and innumeracy and a frustrating life at home and away. Betty Lou also claimed she had been raped by her father in early childhood, as well as sexually abused by others. By the age of twelve her family life was falling apart. Her mother had been institutionalized due to breakdowns caused by alcoholism and Betty Lou had to drop out of school so she could care for her younger brother and sister. Her father, who seemed to see her as a surrogate mother for her siblings, became guarded against any sign of Betty Lou escaping and would beat her for not taking full responsibility for her siblings. She was often at the doctor's office or in hospital for the injuries he inflicted on her. She finally left school completely. The family moved to Hampton, Virginia, while Betty Lou was still a young girl, so that her father could work as a machinist. They were poor, she was young and disabled and she was a victim at the hands of the very people who were supposed to care for her. These circumstances were hardly the healthiest for the young girl to grow up in, and it is not shocking that Betty Lou became increasingly unstable and inclined to criminality in such an environment during such a time of deprivation. However it is also noteworthy that many more people suffered equal or worse hardship, yet did not turn to criminal activity. Perhaps it was the combination of everything, all together at once, but as she grew up something was going very, very wrong inside Betty Lou.

At the age of fifteen she married her first husband, Robert Franklin Branson. Far from an age where anyone feels quite ready to move into adulthood, Betty Lou was married for the first time. She would remain with him for seventeen years before finally divorcing. Although she levied accusations of violence against all her husbands, Robert Franklin Branson was the only one whose life she did not threaten directly herself. It appears he picked up where her father left off. If she was ever a unilateral victim, this may have been the one time. Within the first year she attempted suicide and became pregnant. They had a daughter together. She also later had a son with Robert Branson, who was also named Robert after his father. They went onto have four more children. Their children may have been a factor in reducing the marital violence, extending the duration of the relationship and, ultimately, saving Robert Branson Senior's life. In 1958 he evicted her from their home and put her on a bus to Virginia while he kept her children, at which point Betty again attempted suicide via an overdose of sleeping pills. They divorced in 1969, which left Betty Lou a financial and emotional wreck.

Being single took its toll on Betty Lou. She attached her self-worth to her ability to stay married. She began drinking to fight her feelings of loneliness. Between her own insecurities and the hard time she had getting money from either Robert Branson or the Welfare service to support her, Betty Lou soon felt she needed to remarry. She married Billy York Lane at the age of thirty two. Their marriage was a tumultuous one, and very short. There was evidence of mutual violence and disregard for each other's wellbeing. Lane had been abusive towards a previous partner and Betty Lou responded to his violence in turn. Her daughters recall how he used to beat her senseless and how she used to attack him. He initially wanted to charge her for attempted murder, but swiftly dropped the charges after he was forced to admit he had attacked her, broken her nose and threatened her life. They divorced the same year and remarried again shortly after the trial. After Betty Lou shot at him, Billy York Lane divorced her again, only a month after their remarriage, this time for good. It would prove the wisest decision of his life, as her subsequent husbands found out.

Betty Lou remained single for a year and unmarried for eight more years. During the interim Betty Lou worked in a warehouse, then took up work at a topless bar to cover the bills. She sent two of their children back home to Branson, as she could not afford to care for them. She went on to marry Ronnie C. Threlkold, her boyfriend of seven years, at the age of forty. However this relationship would be as unpredictable, violent and dangerous for Ronnie as it was for Billy. In this case there was little evidence Ronnie had been violent towards Betty Lou, although she accused him of violence at later dates, but her habits had been firmly cemented and she continued to display abusive behaviour towards him. She also continued to work at the topless bar, resulting in arrests and thirty days in country jail under the charge of public lewdness. Despite their seven year courtship, the marriage lasted just a year, culminating in Betty Lou Beets's attempted homicide of Ronnie in 1978, where she shot him in the stomach, wounding him, and their divorce in 1979.

She married Doyle Wayne Barker at the age of forty one, closely after her divorce from Threlkold. Their marriage lasted a mere seven weeks before her violent behaviour drove Doyle away from her. However his own violence was undeniable. He had stalked her, assaulted her and raped her during their short relationship. The day he left Betty Lou had bruises all over her face, neck, arms and chest. There is no available record of the divorce, however all living parties assumed it had taken place. However Doyle Wayne did not get out of their marriage unscathed. He disappeared after their divorce and his body was found years later, buried under a garage, killed by three gunshots.

But this grisly deed was not uncovered for many more years to come. Rather, Betty Lou went on to marry a firefighter named Jimmy Don Beets, her final husband, at the age of forty four.

"Jimmy Don Beets was a wonderful man," said a family friend. "He was loved by so many people. An old country boy that a lot people had respect for."

Their courtship would last a mere six months. Betty Lou would meet Jimmy while she worked as a waitress and the seduction began. Her two sons moved in with them. This would be her final marriage, and her actions within it would be her undoing. Although their courtship had been pleasant, they both suffered from alcoholism, which slowly drove their marriage to the same violence she had experienced previously. Less than a year later she murdered him by gunshot, and this time she was caught. Robert Branson, her son from her first marriage, had been informed that she intended to kill her last husband, telling him to steer clear of the residence as the murder took place. On the 6$^{th}$ of August 1983, Robert Branson Junior left their home and Betty Lou Beets committed the gruesome act. Not only did Robert provide evidence that the act was premeditated, but he also was expected to participate. Two hours after leaving the house, Robert Branson Junior returned, finding his step father dead with two gunshot wounds in his body. Rather than seek assistance, Robert Branson Junior, either tainted by a lifetime with a mother who viewed abuse and murder as daily events or himself an individual with low empathy, helped his mother to dispose of the body. Betty Lou Beets and Robert Branson Junior carted Jimmy Don Beets' body outside to an ornamental wishing well that stood in the front yard of their house. Undetected, they cast the body inside.

Then, Betty Lou returned to the house to cover up her acts. She called the police to report her husband missing from their Cedar Creek Lake home. The next day, Betty Lou became more devious. Perhaps inspired, perhaps unnerved by her success killing Doyle Wayne Barker, she realized she needed to create a story with which to divert the police from her trail. Robert Branson Junior recalled to the press how she had taken some of Jimmy Don Beets's heart medication down to his boat at the lake. Then she had removed the propeller, placed the medication in the boat and abandoned it, floating loosely in the water. Later that day, as the twenty four hours since Jimmy Don Beets's initial disappearance drew to a close, various officials began the search for the presumably missing man. Officers from the Henderson County Sheriff's department, various members of the fire department, as well as agents from the Texas Parks and Wildlife department searched for three weeks. They naturally found no body. However they did find Jimmy Don Beets's boat drifting in the lake, near to the Redwood

Beach Marina. There they found his fishing license, an unused life jacket and the heart medication which Betty Lou Beets had placed there. Not knowing anything about the murder or the forged evidence, they brought Betty Lou Beets to the Marina as the sole witness, where she identified the boat and its contents as those of her husband. Although no body had been recovered, it was considered case closed.

Betty Lou Beets would have likely got away with both murders, were it not for confidential information given to the Henderson County Sheriff's Department two years later. The information suggested that Jimmy Don Beets had not disappeared innocently, and that his assumed death, with no body that had been found, may be the result of foul play. The evidence was enough that the cold case was reopened in Spring 1985. As their suspicions became stronger, the investigators were drawn to Betty Lou Beets, who was arrested on the 8th of June of 1985 and then booked into the Henderson County Jail. An officer on the case, Rick Rose, who had been in charge of her arrest warrant, secured a further warrant to search the Beets's home and lands, including the yard. Ultimately, they discovered Jimmy Don Beets's remains buried under the wishing well where he had been left two years prior. But another discovery would surface that would further disturb the case. Also in the back yard was a storage shed which could be moved. When the officers moved it, something compelled them to disturb the soil that had lain there several years. Perhaps it was some confidential evidence or perhaps it was just intuition, but it paid off when they discovered a second body. Doyle Wayne Barker, still missing, was buried there, with three bullets in his body. All five bullets matched the .38 caliber pistol which had been seized from their home after another incident of Betty Lou's violent outbursts. Thanks to the calls she had made the very day of his disappearance there was no room to argue that she had been abusing drugs or alcohol at the time, but there had been no physical evidence that suggested to detectives at the time that Jimmy Don had been abusing her when the incident took place. Her position was weak.

Faced with the evidence, Robert Branson Junior and his sister Shirley finally confessed to their awareness of the killings, as well as their hand in the crimes that had taken place. Not only had Betty Lou told her son about the murder, but she had also informed her daughter, by the Shirley Stegner and not living at the family home, that she planned on killing her husband. Shirley was motivated by her confession to also confess to her involvement in another crime. She told the detectives that she had been involved in the burial of Doyle Wayne Barker's body in October of 1981 after Betty Lou had shot him to death.

In an effort to make herself more likeable to the jury, Betty Lou Beets raised her history of domestic violence as an excuse for her violent behaviour, levying charges against all her prior husbands, as well as her father. However, this would be the first that anyone had heard of most of these charges. This may have been due to attitudes of the times, a desire to protect her children, or the apparently two-sided nature of most of these incidents, however the jury would not believe her claims. They were just too convenient. Instead, it was clear to them that Betty Lou Beets was an unstable and dangerous woman and the only connection between the five men she married and their violence. Whatever the situation was, her psychological well being was never considered during the trial. Despite the obvious impact her upbringing and life would have on her mental state and the fact that her actions up until that point were indicative of definite mental illness, the trial system of the time did not account for that.

Furthermore, the premeditated nature of her actions was evident through her children's abundant testimonials, where they confessed she had shared her intent to kill not only the husbands she managed to murder, but that she had expressed a desire to kill all the men she had been married to. Not only that, but her success concealing the bodies, under the wishing well and under the garden shed, showed a lack of remorse and serious consideration of her crimes. However it seems Betty Lou had not been as careful as she thought. As soon as the trial began, various other witnesses emerged to testify against her. Various people recalled her attempting to collect life insurance of over a hundred thousand dollars as well as a pension of over a thousand dollars a month after Jimmy Don's declared death. A year after the official death of Jimmy Don Beets, she successfully sold his boat, the primary evidence that he had disappeared. She claimed she did not know about his pension or insurance, however seeing as Jimmy Don Beets was already retired and claiming his pension, this claim fell short. Furthermore, had she no awareness of them she would not have pursued either so actively. She claimed she had been told about them when she visited an attorney by the name or E. Ray Andrews about a fire insurance claim she needed to make, at which point he discovered she could claim his insurance and pension. However her own filing for these benefits did not align with the supposed visit, and the only person who could say for sure that she had not known about her deceased husband's finances was E. Ray Andrews himself, who agreed to represent her in exchange for the rights to book and movie deals concerning her life and case.

Betty Lou Beets was indicted for murder for remuneration or the promise of remuneration, with her recovery of his life insurance and pension as evidence. She plead not guilty and was taken to trial, where she was found guilty of the capital offence of first degree murder on the 11<sup>th</sup> of October of 1985. She was found again guilty during a hearing on the 14<sup>th</sup> of October 1985 and was sentenced to death by the trial court. This was due to her prior history of violence and attempted murders, which suggested that she would present a threat to others in the future, specifically to any man who entered a relationship with her again. Yet her conviction and sentence were quickly and successfully appealed to the Texas Court of Criminal Appeals. Such was the situation that, under Texas law, crime for the sake of insurance and pension claims was not covered by the definition of "murder for remuneration", instead falling into two separate categories of first degree murder and insurance fraud, or crime with intent to commit insurance fraud. The Texas Court of Criminal Appeals reversed her conviction for capital murder, citing the Texas Penal Code as evidence that her particular case could not be filed as "murder for remuneration". The State then requested a rehearing of the cause. Although her original conviction had been overturned, the fact remained that Betty Lou Beets was guilty of homicide under some circumstance or another.

On the 21$^{st}$ of September of 1988, the Court of Criminal Appeals reinstated her conviction and sentence based on the evidence received. Betty Lou Beets was on death row. Her execution was scheduled for the 8$^{th}$ of November 1989.

However her court case did not go as it should have in the first place. Attorney E. Ray Andrews was heavily invested in sensationalizing her case as much as he could, seeing as he would profit enormously from the case blowing up into a media phenomenon. So although she claimed and he later agreed that she had known nothing of her husband's finances, the trial was conducted under the assumption that she was fully aware of the money she would receive. Not only that, but E. Ray Andrews did everything in his power to create a more dramatic case on both sides, which ultimately meant excluding Betty Lou from much of the information about her own trial. Betty Lou was becoming desperate at this point. Although she had a long history of domestic violence, attempted murder and two bodies in her garden, she decided to attempt to blame the murder of Jimmy Don Beets on Robert Branson Junior, her own son. She did not seem to have made the statement in sound mind, but E. Ray Andrews allowed her to speak on her own behalf and did not retract it, as it added dramatic quality to the event. He tried to cover up later, saying that Betty Lou had possibly been taking the blame for her son, however he had no proof other than that Robert Branson Junior was male and from a rough background. This statement and its acceptance horrified the court, as it was alarming to them to see a mother who, rather than protect her children, was willing to throw them under the bus by falsely accusing them of a crime she had more than evidently committed. Furthermore, by admitting and adhering to the story that Robert Branson Junior was in fact the actual killer, Betty Lou lost all chances of arguing that she acted in self-defence and made her own accusations of domestic violence against Jimmy Don and her prior husbands completely irrelevant. This is despite the fact that a leading domestic violence specialist of the time believed Betty Lou Beets had been significantly mentally impacted by her experiences, and that she suffered "the emotional, cognitive, and behavioural components of battered woman syndrome, rape trauma syndrome, and PTSD" which he added must have interacted with her pre-existing organic brain damage from her childhood illness, history of battering and substance abuse. All together, this would have presented a robust case for her mental illness and need for treatment rather than punishment. However E. Ray Andrews discarded this option in favour of the more dramatic choice of supporting Betty Lou's accusation against her son. They became stuck in the position of having to argue she did not kill her husband at all. This context may have reduced her sentence, or made her eligible to claim insanity. However neither of these options were available.

Throughout the entire case, E. Ray Andrews failed to represent her seriously and did nothing to prevent her from shooting herself in the foot repeatedly. In fact, seeing the case was a lost cause and that he stood to gain more from her sentence than her freedom, Andrews began drinking heavily for the duration of the trial. He chose not to bear witness to her claims that she did not know about Jimmy Don Beets's pension or insurance, which would have transformed the case to one of murder in the context of domestic violence, rather than murder for remuneration. He managed to offer the jury no reasons to consider that Betty Lou was not a serious threat to those around her, eventually sealing her fate. Yet he remained her attorney for the duration of her appeal as well. It was he who raised the point that her financial gain was not necessarily the motivator for murder, but a by product. He also finally raised that she was not aware of the insurance or pension until she spoke to him, however this was met with scepticism due to his negligence to mention it any sooner, and was perceived as a lie in effort to overturn Betty Lou's criminal charges after his initial failure to protect her.

On the 16<sup>th</sup> of October 1989, Betty Lou filed a motion called a stay of execution which would delay her execution to give her time to prepare and file a habeas corpus application with the state. On the 1<sup>st</sup> of November she filed the application and the trial court delayed her execution so that the claims she was raising, such as consideration towards her mental state and marital conditions, could be properly addressed. During this time Betty Lou wrote several letters from prison in which she attempted to defend her good name and that of her last husband. She attempted to balance the accusations that she was a black widow by reminding the court that she was Jimmy Don's fourth wife as well. However his previous wives did not come forward to support her. She also defended her own identity, denying that she ever worked as a barmaid, regardless of her own charges for lewd behaviour, and that she was never on welfare, despite her claims after her first divorce. She also said that the Fire Department Chaplain, who stated he had informed her about Beets's insurance and pension, had spoken to her sister in law, Betty Beets, instead. She even quibbled over the descriptions of her garden, insisting the well was a planter in the shape of a well and not an actual well. It was clear that Betty Lou Beets was desperate to save face and project a more pleasant, more ordinary identity than the one which E. Ray Andrews had created for her in the courtroom. It was also clear that her mental health was degrading as she endured life in prison and submitted her habeas corpus petition. In her petition she argued against her sentence of the death penalty, raising issues such as the alleged value Jimmy Don Beets apparently added the community, the testimonials of victims and sufferers whose statements were unconstitutional under the Victim Impact Statements act of 1987, and the poor assistance which E. Ray Andrews provided, especially regarding her history of domestic abuse. Yet without his help in writing and presenting the letter, her claims were weak and not fully backed by legal evidence. Andrews did not visit her from the point of her sentencing and prepared for her trials without ever speaking to her. Furthermore, she could have claimed that his services were provided against American Bar Association rules, which prohibit the trade of legal services for copyright issues, such as the rights to her case. None of this was raised by her against him, and as such it was not considered during her habeas corpus appeal.

However on the 27th of June her appeal for state habeas corpus was turned away. She was placed in the position of proving that, had E. Ray Andrews presented a testimony about her lack of awareness of the insurance and her history of domestic violence, the jury would have judged her not guilty of a capital crime. Without a proper attorney to defend her, it would be impossible for Betty Lou to prove this was the case, and the court deemed Andrews's mistakes to have been harmless to her trial. The Fifth Circuit Court of Appeals went on to turn down her final appeals. The judges remained convinced that, regardless of any remaining evidence, Betty Lou Beets's history of violence and attempted murder, along with the two concealed bodies in her garden, were evidence enough that a death sentence was a fair response to the crime that had taken place. She had displayed violence her whole life, even towards men who had not presented a threat to her, and had attempted to kill all but one of her husbands. She had concealed her murders carefully and for many years and was willing to place the blame on her own adult son. In other words, regardless of her own situation, her criminal intent was viewed as evident and incorrigible, and her death sentence was the only fitting end to her crime spree.

On death row, Betty Lou Beets retained some supporters, mostly her own children. Some of Betty Lou's daughters went to E. Ray Andrews with photographic evidence of the domestic abuse she had suffered in order to request a parole review, but were declined. They insisted on presenting the evidence that she had suffered and that her acts of violence were a result of brain damage and abuse, not of malicious intent. Faye Lane, one of her daughters, insisted that her mother would only have done anything so horrific if she believed she was abused. Domestic violence awareness groups and charities acting against the death sentence appealed to have her sentence changed to a life sentence in prison, based not only on her own suffering, but on their universal stance against the irreversible process of the death penalty. Yet even those defending her maintained that she was a violent, unpredictable woman and not safe to exit into the general public.

And not all her children were so kind. Shirley told the press that Doyle Wayne Barker was killed because he owned the trailer where they lived, and that after the divorce which Barker had initiated, Betty Lou and her children would be evicted from the trailer and left homeless. This set a precedent where even her own daughter could not believe that Betty Lou was completely unaware of the financial benefits of murdering Jimmy Don Beets, especially not after she had successfully killed Barker. Knowing that she was still doubted and seeing hope as ever distant, Betty Lou composed her memoirs from death row, presenting her case.

Beets turned to her last resort which was to appeal to then-governor George W. Bush to spare her life. After a media incident where he jokingly insulted the last woman to be executed in Texas in an insensitive manner, George W. Bush seemed keen to prove he had no bias against women, even in the prison system, and agreed to review her case. This would have meant hearing the witnesses which had not been heard by the trial lawyer and present a case against her execution based on the circumstances of her life, including medical and psychiatric evidence. He could have granted her a thirty day reprieve in which he made his decision, however this never materialized. His number was made available and he received thousands of calls and letters from people urging him to spare her, with only fifty seven endorsing her sentence. Yet he did not grant the reprieve or halt the execution.

Betty Lou Beets was finally executed on the 24th of February of 2000, via lethal injection. Protestors from various organisations gathered outside as her sentence awaited. She declined both her last meal and her final statement, having been given by then enough time to make sense of what was happening and to say everything which needed to be said. Strapped to the death chamber gurney, she received her injection at six pm and died within eighteen minutes. She was sixty two years old. She left behind five adult children, nine grandchildren and six great-grandchildren, as well as her memoirs. Her story may be shocking, and it may be hard to pick sides at times, but that is exactly why her trial presents a solid case against the black and white ideals the court system held regarding crime and punishment, perpetrator and victim, defence and offence. Someone can at once be a victim of horrific crimes and a perpetrator of them, at once be a defendant and raise accusations, at once deserve punishment yet suffer a crime gone unpunished. There is no doubt that Betty Lou Beets was a violent woman who invited violence into her own life, an alcoholic and a murderer. However there is no doubt either that she was a good mother within her capacity, a victim of a series of horrific crimes, a disabled person with a background she could not escape and a desperate woman who saw no way out of her situation. Neither black nor white, good not bad, Betty Lou Beets sits in the grey areas of the law.